CREATING
PATHS
OF
CHANGE

D1595209

CREATING
PATHS
OF
CHANGE

MANAGING ISSUES AND RESOLVING
PROBLEMS IN ORGANIZATIONS

SECOND PRINTING

WILL MCWHINNEY, PH.D.

JAMES B. WEBBER
DOUGLAS M. SMITH
BERNIE J. NOVOKOWSKY

SAGE Publications
International Educational and Professional Publisher
Thousand Oaks   London   New Delhi

For information address:

SAGE Publications, Inc.
2455 Teller Road
Thousand Oaks, California 91320
E-mail: order@sagepub.com

SAGE Publications Ltd.
6 Bonhill Street
London EC2A 4PU
United Kingdom

SAGE Publications India Pvt. Ltd.
M-32 Market
Greater Kailash I
New Delhi 110 048 India

Printed in the United States of America

Library of Congress Cataloging-in-Publication Data

Creating paths of change : managing issues and resolving problems in
    organizations / Will McWhinney ... [et al.]. — 2nd ed.
        p.   cm.
    Includes bibliographical references.
    ISBN 0-7619-1007-7 (pbk. : acid-free paper)
    1. Organizational change.   I. McWhinney, Will.
HD58.8.C72   1997
658.4'06—dc21   97-4640

This book is printed on acid-free paper.

97 98 99 00 01 02 10 9 8 7 6 5 4 3 2 1

The first edition of this book was originally published in 1993, by Enthusion, Inc.

WORDS OF APPRECIATION

The idea for this guide book originated when Doug Smith and Bernie Novokowsky suggested that the concepts in *Paths of Change* could be turned into tools for achieving every-day change that occurs within our work places and communities. Together with Jim Webber, they wrote the first version of this guide book and tested it in their practices. We expanded it into a published first edition for an IBM training course, with the enthusiasm and contributions of Eleanor McCulley. This first edition has been widely used by individual managers, community volunteers, organizational consultants, and in courses at a number of universities.

The second edition has taken its form under the editorship and graphic design of Diana Price. She clarified text, designed illustrations and charts, and researched the alternatives that brought the book into its current form. She worked with Bonnie McWhinney and myself to preserve the aesthetic values and user-friendliness of the first edition, increasing the symmetry and consistency that is essential in a guide book. We also incorporated new Tools of Change, expanded the discussions, and, most importantly, responded to the practitioners and researchers who were using this material in the field. Feedback from users of the first edition has been incorporated into the second edition. New ideas also came from a number of graduates at the Fielding Institute, particularly through the doctoral research of Tamara Bliss and Nancy Lapelle. I am also thankful for the thought provoking conversations I had with Ian Mitroff and Tom Greening.

The illustrations are from many sources, but I wish to particularly acknowledge my admiration for the German anti-war artist and cartoonist, A. Paul Webber. One of his metaphorical drawings of chess games is reproduced here. The etching explores the subtle meaning and humor of the many games we play.

Will McWhinney

CONTENTS

INTRODUCTION

THE REASONS I AM READING THIS BOOK ARE TO:

Know the best ways of solving problems.	Locate the most efficient tools.
Ground my understanding in theory.	Do more with less.
Assure that I am using procedures correctly.	Improve my supervisory skills.
Make proper use of resources.	Teach new methods of problem solving and resolving conflicts to others.
Clarify the mission.	Solve a problem.
Find expression for my ideas.	Improve my facilitation skills.
"Cliff note" my problem-solving efforts.	Work with people better.
Catapult me into futuristic and inventive approaches.	Understand others' ways.
Better enjoy my work.	Find new processes to enhance team performance.
Create visions.	Be clear about my values.

Find yourself on this chart. Circle the reasons that are strongest for you. Are they located mostly in one or two quadrants? Chapter 1 discusses the patterns shown in your selections.

INTRODUCTION

Individuals, organizations, and communities constantly engage in change. We choose to make changes out of our desperations and sympathies, out of the awareness of opportunities, and for the pure joy of exercising our skills. Some changes are simple adjustments in daily routines, some require the resolution of conflicts, and others require extensive programs of redesign and reevaluation. All change calls for ingenuity and wisdom in responding to the needs of co-workers, clients, and friends. *Creating Paths of Change* guides you through effective paths of change to manage and resolve issues. It is written for individuals and groups—managers, entrepreneurs, parents, and consultants—who are taking responsibility for the change effort. It addresses the problems you face in the daily operations of organizational life, and provides a foundation and theory for effective and sustained issue resolution.

Frequently, change does not solve problems adequately because we do not understand the consequences or inadequacies of our own actions. Unfortunately, the same problems keep coming back, sometimes just as they were before the change; but more frequently with the additional entanglement of other issues. We need approaches that help us select the paths and tools for change, enabling us to sustain results, settle differences, and reduce the stress of life in our terribly turbulent world. Achieving successful results is increasingly difficult and requires more skill and knowledge, and less dependence on rules of thumb and past successes. Our ability to choose effective paths of change must be based in knowing not only theories of technology, economics, organizational relations, and human behavior, but also in understanding models and theories of change. Good theories provide a basis for reflection and enable us to learn from our successes and failures. Theories also enable us to better respond to a diverse range of situations and better anticipate the consequences of our actions. Nothing is more practical than a good theory.

"We believe that you can best initiate change by looking at yourself."

"You are the initiator of change. How you view the world is a critical element in defining your decisions."

Creating Paths of Change is based on a theory of change and resolution. This theory has been tested explicitly over the last two decades, as described in McWhinney's *Paths of Change* (1992). However, the concepts of world views and grand paths of change are of ancient origins. They have been used world wide over the centuries—from sources as diverse as the Navaho healing process, Jungian depth psychology, the study of social revolution, and many models taught in contemporary business practices. *Creating Paths of Change* provides both the models of the change process and the tools for applying these models.

OUR APPROACH

Creating Paths of Change provides you with a powerful process to *get things done*. Before acting we believe you should take a step back and look at yourself. You are the *initiator* of change. How you view the world is a critical element in defining your decisions. When evaluating problems, your decisions may vastly differ from the decisions of other people. Different initiators will have differing approaches. To make changes effectively it is important that you understand that these world views and attitudes toward change are characteristics of *you*, the initiator. Clarifying your world views and the attitudes of your co-workers will aid you in choosing a path toward resolution. Our approach teaches you how to select a path of change that suits **you** as the initiator of actions, together with the available **resources** and the **presenting problem** you collectively confront.

Taking the right steps toward solving a problem depends on having the particular skills appropriate to the situation. You need to first identify and understand your own world views and attitudes toward change. You then search for resources, people, money, and situations that match your image of what it will take to work the larger issue. In participation with your new team you reexamine yourselves and your assets, then repeat the assessment of the situation. Only now can you define the problem and organize your resources into a coherent force. When

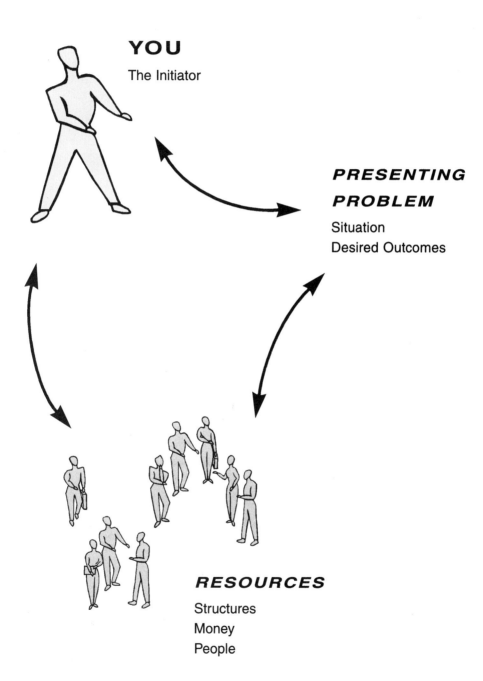

YOU
The Initiator

PRESENTING
PROBLEM
Situation
Desired Outcomes

RESOURCES
Structures
Money
People

your team has found itself, it is time to begin formulating a path of change.

This guide book creates the paths of change that you as problem solvers may travel. It provides general rules that will allow you to work in any territory, solving problems and resolving conflicts wherever you identify them. The theory of change we introduce provides a fresh language for understanding the roles of the participants in the problem, as well as providing powerful processes through which change can be achieved and conflicts resolved.

We guide you through the *Modes of Change* according to your world views and describe strategies for dealing with the problems along a path of change. We reveal the relationship between the Modes of Change and the *Leadership Styles*, and how leaders and followers interact in the processes of change. You learn how to choose paths and strategies for change, preparing you for deciding which tool is appropriate for your situation. *The Tools of Change* provide step-by-step descriptions of problem solving processes, identifying where they fit into a path of change and the characteristics of people who might best utilize that tool.

Even how you use this book is contingent upon your style of approaching work. Once you have identified your dominant Realities in Chapter 1, you may read the chapters in any sequence you wish. We have organized the book to give you freedom to use your own style. The path you take is likely to be a customary expression of your world view. With reading and practice you will gain the knowledge and confidence to surpass your initial comfort zone, using your resources and solving problems more efficiently.

CHAPTER 1

You, The Agent of Change

INITIATING CHANGE

"To see problems clearly and recognize possible solutions you must understand yourself as the instrument who defines the problem."

One person's perception of the problem and its solutions may be completely different from another's.

You initiate change by taking action. As an agent of change, you must face the question "How do I initiate changes that will effectively manage an issue?" To define the issue and a path to its solution requires that you begin with yourself. Who am I? How do I view the world? What resources and skills do I command? How do I habitually solve issues? To see problems clearly and recognize possible solutions you must understand yourself as the instrument who defines the problem.

The function and motivation of someone in the role of a change agent depends upon their world views. Change agents can be managers implementing a mandated program, facilitators aiding others who have taken on a change effort, or consultants to executives. They can be foresters choosing what trees to cut or parents selecting a treatment for a sick child. Whatever the role, someone has to take responsibility for the first step.

Those attempting to solve problems must develop tactics for defining problems as well as tactics for determining and implementing solutions. People formulate problems based on how they view the world. This world view determines what they perceive as the primary problem, its fundamental cause, and the potential solutions. One person's perception of the problem and its solutions may be completely different from another's. Only you as an initiator and manager of change can define what will solve the problems that you face. You must recognize your own role in creating the problem and the accompanying conflicts.

MANAGING THE CONFLICT YOU CREATE

Conflict is the companion to change and the resolution of issues. All change produces imbalance in our environment even when done in the service of restoring balance and solving issues. People in conflict do not necessarily have ill intentions or even opposing goals. All significant and successful problem solving requires the management of conflict. It is a consideration in every one of the problem solving methods that we discuss in this book.

Conflict management, problem solving, and issue resolution are various forms of change activities. We use the language of "problems" and "issues" when we fantasize that the resolution process will go smoothly. We generally use the term "conflict" when open conflict is a presenting symptom or when we sense that the solution will take us into large interpersonal or societal issues. Obviously, the tools we employ when we acknowledge open conflict will be different than those we use when facing the diverse views in a long term urban development or the design of a new computer. Every choice must take into account the need to manage conflict. This book identifies the particular paths of change and the tools we should use whether we treat an issue as a problem or a conflict.

DETERMINING "WHAT IS REAL"

"The world is, after all, a certain way." That is what people tend to assume and how they respond when communicating with friends or facing challenges in their environment. We solve problems and determine paths of change based on our concept of how we think the world works, what is *real* to us. People successfully apply many differing concepts about what is real and how to interact with others. Your version of Reality may be strikingly different from your teammates or opponents. Most small differences get smoothed over with customary pleasantries: "Excuse me," "I hope you don't mind," and "It really doesn't matter." We develop these customs, agree to be nice to each other, and not challenge each other's fundamental beliefs. When people hold strikingly different fundamental assumptions about what is real, even the simplest changes can lead to conflict and prevent resolution.

Determining what people believe is real enables us to better understand each other and resolve the resulting conflicts. Fortunately, these differing beliefs are associated with a distinct set of world views. Grouping people according to their typical patterns of beliefs allows us to understand their responses, and better anticipate their actions. Many current studies suggest that we can make good distinctions by grouping beliefs into a set of four different world views. This will give us enough appreciation of the differences to work most issues effectively. We present here a set of four world views based on *Paths of Change* (1992), by Will McWhinney. It provides a clear set of patterns which match what we see in people around us. Informally you can identify people's preferred world views by examining the way they behave. You can use the questionnaire, *The Reality Inquiry*, printed at the end of this chapter to get a more reliable measure. Use it to evaluate the relative strengths of the four Realities for yourself and others.

THE FOUR REALITIES

Important differences between people and their behaviors can be described with four different world views. These four views help us understand how differently people approach resolving conflict and managing issues. How we view Reality not only defines how we solve problems but characterizes our styles of leadership and creativity as well. They also indicate how well a group's world view matches different styles of organization and consequently indicate what paths will accomplish their goals. In addition, the four Realities reveal aspects of our personalities as do specific personality typologies such as the Myers-Briggs Type Indicator, the Kolb Learning Style Indicator, and the brain dominance instruments.

The labels we attach to these four world views may be new to you but the ideas have been around for centuries in every culture. People in Medieval Europe called them the humors; Jung calls them archetypes. Oriental cultures identified the four ways of being with the four directions; American Indians refer to the four winds. We intend that you recognize the four world views as a systemization of wisdom from many cultures.

You will likely find concepts with which you identify within each of the four Realities: Unitary, Sensory, Social, and Mythic. Some Realities may be noticeably more kindred to you than others, revealing initial preferences and rejections. Your responses to "The reasons I am reading this book" in the Introduction give clues to your Reality views. The following pages examine your Reality preferences in more detail.

MY BELIEFS ARE MOST LIKE:

Policies	Actions
Rules	Behaviors
Theories	Facts
Truths	Data
Creeds	Objects
Principles	Material Things
Designs	Resources
Belief Systems	Events
Clarifications	Experience
Assumptions	Sensuality

UNITARY | **SENSORY**

MYTHIC | **SOCIAL**

Visions	Values
Ideas	Feelings
Symbols	Preferences
Meanings	What Matters
Opportunities	Purposes
Metaphors	Wants
Dreams	Motivations
Inventions	Ethics
Inspirations	Attitudes
Creations	Appreciation

YOUR WORLD VIEWS

Everyone comes into adulthood with a particular set of preferences. You become attached to a preferred world view and its Reality becomes a part of your personality. Differences in our Realities become apparent when looking at a few simple characteristics.

WHAT IS THE MOST REAL FOR YOU?

This must seem obvious—you know what is real. Although for one person Reality is what she senses, for another it is what he cares about, for another, it is what he believes. Different people focus on different Realities.

HOW DO THINGS USUALLY HAPPEN?

Again this seems obvious, but my arguments will be different from many of yours. People have different explanations for events, and these explanations follow along with their Reality preferences.

HOW ARE YOU ABOUT ACCEPTING CHANGE?

For some people, change happens; for others, it is what they make happen. The differences are important to us—they are major causes of all our interpersonal conflicts.

These characteristics, and how they vary, are examined in the tables on the following pages.

WHAT IS MOST REAL FOR YOU?

TRUTHS

Unitary Reality takes as most fundamental a set of truths such as the existence of God, science and numbers, a set of ethical rules of behavior, the American constitution, and local truths such as "My father taught me I must be good to my mother." Things do not exist independently; they are defined according to principles and rules.

FACTS

Sensory Reality takes as given the impressions received through the senses—"seeing is believing." (So is feeling, smelling, hearing and tasting.) This world view accepts the Reality of space and time and the distinctness of things. It is the Reality of our rational behavior.

UNITARY | SENSORY

MYTHIC | SOCIAL

IDEAS

Mythic Reality invents the world. It is the Reality of ideas, dreams, plans, hopes, and their expression in art work, inventions, organizations, and cultures. It brings something into being by beliefs and actions. By naming and symbolizing, we create objects that have not been "seen" before.

FEELINGS

Social Reality recognizes only that which matters. "If it doesn't matter it doesn't exist." In this belief, whatever exists for us is created by one or more people caring about it. It is Social in that values are created by the intentions of groups of people.

HOW DO THINGS USUALLY HAPPEN?

BY FORM

Unitary Reality holds that an event follows the logic that orders our lives—events follow the customs or principles of how we do things. For example, we drive on the right simply as a common form; doing so simplifies life. The law of gravity is but a principle; it follows the form the universe has taken.

BY PRECEDENCE

Sensory Reality holds that things are caused by what has happened before or concurrently. Everything must have a cause and conversely everything causes something. This is the Reality of empirical sciences and history and we use it when we are fixing our cars and seasoning our food.

UNITARY | SENSORY

MYTHIC | SOCIAL

BY CREATING

Mythic Reality assumes that people have the power to create the experienced world and every one in it. Consequently, they take credit and bear responsibility for everything that happens.

BY INTENDING

Social Reality accepts the idea that people make things happen intentionally. They have a purpose, an aim in their actions. This is a belief in humanity's freedom to work toward making things happen that they care about. This is the Reality of social construction; "it" appears in a particular way because we wanted it to.

HOW ARE YOU ABOUT ACCEPTING CHANGE?

NO BASIC CHANGE

Unitary beliefs do not include any acceptance of change. They allow for no change in the modern sense, only reinterpretation of established principles and the deductions that follow from these principles. Accepting that many people hold this belief will help you understand the widely experienced resistance to change.

UNITARY

NO UNCAUSED CHANGE

Sensory Reality does not believe people have control over change. Change occurs based on what happened in the past, and is restrained by current technology. What is going to happen, is going to happen. This is the dogma of the scientific age as expressed by planners, supervisors, and those who repair our cars.

SENSORY

MYTHIC

SOCIAL

"EVERYTHING WAS AND IS AS I WILL IT"

Mythic Reality believes there is no change because whatever is perceived at the moment is the way the world is. A Mythic person's world is not subject to rules or limited by data of earlier times and places. Observers may see the Mythic's world as completely unstable and even more unpredictable than that of the Social Reality.

FULLY ACCEPT CHANGE

Social Reality accepts ongoing change as human beings express their feelings, which modifies what is real. A varying mixture of people's needs will produce a change in values, and thus changes in the perception of Reality.

YOUR REALITY PREFERENCES

As you see, we all have our Reality preferences and specific styles of working that reflect what we believe is real. These preferences remain relatively stable over the course of our lives. We tend to use the same predictable reasoning skills in all types of situations—making choices, leading others, and following leaders. We become naturally more skilled in one style of work and generally avoid dealing with people whose styles conflicts with our own.

If you know your own preferences and avoidances you can more easily understand which "Tools of Change" are best for you, which tools you should get someone to help you use, and which are clearly out of your range of effective use. This knowledge is an essential component of effective problem solving, managing and leading, and of all interpersonal engagements. Your exploration of your own preferences will give you a personal understanding of the ideas and suggestions made in this book.

By this point, you may have gained a clear idea of your preferences among the Realities, especially if you have a strong favorite. Nevertheless, you may find it useful to get a "second opinion" by completing the questionnaire called *The Reality Inquiry*. Getting a reading of your score will help you reflect more accurately on your preferences and styles of work. It will also help you to be more aware and understanding of how differently other people may feel, think, and speak.

The Reality Inquiry questionnaire is reproduced on the following pages with instructions for completing, scoring, and interpreting it. We encourage you to photocopy it so that others in your immediate world can also complete it. However, we request that you contact the authors if you wish to use the inquiry extensively with employees in an organization or with clients.

REALITY INQUIRY

The *Reality Inquiry* indicates the *Modes of Change* which you are mostly likely to be comfortable using and the *Leadership Styles* that are most natural to you. It forecasts how you make choices and what styles you will exhibit. The inquiry provides data on how well you will match up to a particular task or assignment. There are no better or worse Realities. It is not a clinical judgment of who you are but a projection of how your beliefs and habits can be characterized.

The Inquiry takes 30-40 minutes to complete, and consists of two sections: writing and answering a questionnaire. Do the entire inquiry in a single sitting. Your responses will be more accurate if you answer the survey questions immediately upon completing the writing. Please write or type legibly.

Before you start writing, take time to settle comfortably into your chair, put away distractions, and relax. Take a few deep breaths.

In your mind's eye picture two characters. You can make them up or you can think of people you know. One should be a **leader**, a person you might call a president, king or queen, manager—choose anyone who comes to mind. The other person should be a person of wisdom whom you might want to call a **sage**, a counselor, an earth mother.

Once you establish these characters in your mind and you feel that you know how they would think and behave, write about some sort of encounter that they might have or a situation they might be in together. Write anything you want and use any form you like—a dialogue, a story, stream of consciousness. It need not be particularly long, clever, or polished.

Take at least twenty minutes to write, more if you like. Use the following page for your writing or use your own paper if you wish. When you finish go immediately to the questionnaire and respond to all the questions.

_____

_____

_____

_____

_____

_____

_____

_____

_____

_____

_____

_____

_____

_____

_____

_____

_____

_____

_____

_____

_____

_____

_____

**PLEASE DO NOT READ THE QUESTIONNAIRE UNTIL
YOU HAVE COMPLETED YOUR WRITING.**

REALITY INQUIRY QUESTIONNAIRE

As you respond to these questions, stay connected to the feelings and thoughts you had as you were writing. Remember to think of yourself as the "Author," when answering questions.

Each of the questions on the following pages has four possible responses. Rank the responses by how closely they match your thinking. Put a "1" next to the response that matches your thoughts most closely. Then select the response that is furthest from matching your thinking and rank it "4." Compare the remaining two options and give them rank orderings of "2" and "3."

Please do not have any ties! Each of the four responses to a question must get a ranking different from the others for accurate scoring. If you find yourself thinking that two items rank the same, look again. Chances are that you do not feel exactly the same about them.

SAMPLE QUESTION:

1. When filing out a questionnaire...
   - _4_ a. I take it as a challenge.
   - _1_ b. I sort of enjoy doing it.
   - _3_ c. I struggle with some answers.
   - _2_ d. I always wish it were longer.

QUESTIONNAIRE:

My name:_____

The names, roles, or titles of the two characters I wrote about are:

Leader:_____   Sage:_____

I identify most with (circle one):

Leader   Sage   Neither   Both

1. The dominant feeling I have as I reflect upon my writing is...
    ___ a. I have a sense of well-being, of constructiveness, from having organized a good description.
    ___ b. I feel playful at having begun a more or less ingenious tale.
    ___ c. I'm continuing to think about the characters and their interactions.
    ___ d. I'm pleased to have a chance to write about my world.

2. My writing is about...
    ___ a. the characters working with problems of change.
    ___ b. the way things are.
    ___ c. people making something happen.
    ___ d. a set of facts or a projection into the future.

3. On being asked to write this piece...
    ___ a. I found it thought-provoking to get inside the characters' heads to see how they would behave.
    ___ b. I wanted to write about things and people staying as close to the facts as possible.
    ___ c. I enjoyed creating characters who did what I wanted them to do.
    ___ d. I chose to write about something that's much the way the world is.

4. The piece of writing I just did...
    ___ a. is a story as I would like it to happen.
    ___ b. is about the way the world operates.
    ___ c. seemed to develop naturally from the personalities and situation I selected.
    ___ d. is about tension between people who want to act one way but must, of necessity, act another.

5. If I think about sources of knowledge, I would say that...
    ___ a. all knowledge comes from the senses, either directly by observation or indirectly from one's studies.
    ___ b. the answers to our questions about the universe are all there, waiting to be revealed.
    ___ c. knowledge can come from observation, although, often, what one sees depends heavily on what one wants to see.
    ___ d. people, particularly people like artists, scientists, and political leaders, create knowledge.

6. I think that ideal communication...
    ___ a. results in a community of shared understanding about the universe.
    ___ b. informs the world of my thinking and feeling so as to create understanding and agreement.
    ___ c. comes from presenting one's own views in such a way as to evoke awareness in others.
    ___ d. involves a full exchange of ideas, data, feelings, etc.

7. I think a leader's prime strength lies in...
    ___ a. the authority that's gained by being especially in tune with the purposes and goals of a group.
    ___ b. the authority that derives from deep knowledge of a situation and an understanding of the consequences of alternative actions.
    ___ c. personal charisma, the ability to generate a sense of direction and confidence among one's followers.
    ___ d. the ability to build an environment of mutual confidence and respect among followers.

8. The writing I did pursues the question...
    ____ a. Why? What was the underlying purpose of the problem or situation?
    ____ b. Who? Who had the power to cause some particular events to happen?
    ____ c. What actually happened?
    ____ d. How? What caused the events to happen?

9. People I identify most with...
    ____ a. take the world as it is.
    ____ b. enjoy creating the situations they are in.
    ____ c. get meaning from developing and changing themselves.
    ____ d. get meaning from seeing their efforts being effective.

10. My writing looks at...
    ____ a. the characters working on a problem.
    ____ b. the balance of power in the world of the two characters.
    ____ c. people carrying out tasks which must be done in accordance with a particular structure.
    ____ d. powerful people getting things to happen their way.

11. My idea of a good follower is one who...
    ____ a. is inspired by the leader and is committed to the leader's causes.
    ____ b. defines and expresses himself sufficiently to give the leader a perspective of his skills, needs, and world view.
    ____ c. responds creatively to the opportunities provided by the leader.
    ____ d. can support the leader's work through a shared understanding of a situation and accepts the leader's interpretation when data is missing.

12. Regarding the issues in my writing, I'd say...
    ____ a. they are important ones and express my beliefs.
    ____ b. I"m very much interested in how I made these people act.
    ____ c. my writing describes a situation and the effectiveness of the characters' actions.
    ____ d. my writing explores some moral issue that concerns me.

13. When it comes to making friends...
    ____ a. I seek out friends among people of all types with whom I can exchange feelings and who challenge my ideas.
    ____ b. I make friends with people who are active in the things I am, from whom I can gain opportunities, and to whom I can contribute.
    ____ c. although I work well with people and enjoy good company, there are times when I feel alone, as though I have no friends.
    ____ d. I look to the community of people who share my world views.

14. In the way I think about the world...
    ____ a. the laws by which the world works are rational, all encompassing, and ultimately comprehensible.
    ____ b. there is a vast organization and momentum in the course of nature but we, with great effort, can redirect that course.
    ____ c. to a significant degree we create or choose the worlds we live in.
    ____ d. the world is a fantastic creation that works, whether or not we understand how.

15. When faced with a project to be done...
___ a. I envision it as a challenge and tackle it wholeheartedly.
___ b. I find what is the right way to do it and work accordingly.
___ c. I study the various ways to accomplish it and choose the one most likely to succeed.
___ d. I work with any people who may be involved, try to coordinate needs and activities, and see that we reach our common goal.

16. I feel that all objects, events and people...
___ a. cannot be meaningfully isolated because everyone and everything is part of an indivisible whole.
___ b. are separate but that they do affect each other by their actions or just by their presence.
___ c. are arbitrarily combinable; they are separate but can also be seen as elements of organic wholes.
___ d. can be arbitrarily connected; we can make and break connections in any way we wish.

17. If I were to picture the best future I could, I'd see it produced through...
___ a. the creative minds of people in touch with the deep forces in human nature.
___ b. people looking at varied sources for guidelines but, most importantly—by choosing carefully the means by which we advance into the future.
___ c. projections and descriptions organized by the appropriate sciences.
___ d. identification of the highest ideals.

18. I am very much attracted to...
___ a. understanding people's values.
___ b. getting to know more about people.
___ c. the unexplored abilities and powers of the mind.
___ d. religion or other matters of the spirit.

19. For success in a long term relationship...
___ a. I'd want someone with character and a personality I admire and respect so we'd still love each other after the first glow faded.
___ b. I wouldn't go out and select someone (I will know when someone fits my image), I guess that's what you'd call falling in love.
___ c. I would want a partner who shares my beliefs, values, and background so we would react the same way to life's opportunities and problems.
___ d. I'd want someone always willing to be open about changing needs and feelings so we could both grow within our relationship.

20. If I found or were given a perfectly beautiful stone with a lovely and colorful pattern...
___ a. I would be pleased to have acquired such a wonderful thing; I might value it as sort of a sign or a good luck charm.
___ b. I'd feel joy in knowing that my world can produce such beauty; it could give me a feeling of reverence and connectedness to Nature.
___ c. My pleasure wouldn't be complete until I had learned more about it—what kind of stone it was, where it came from.
___ d. I'd want to display it or wear it so that I could share it with friends.

WHAT IS REAL FOR YOU

Please check back to make sure you have responded to each item and that you have no ties. Enter your rank order number for each question response in the table below. Be sure to put the correct ranking number in the correct Reality column.

Making a copy of this page will make it easier to score the Reality Inquiry.

QUESTION NUMBER	REALITY			
	UNITARY	SENSORY	SOCIAL	MYTHIC
1	___ d	___ a	___ c	___ b
2	___ b	___ d	___ a	___ c
3	___ d	___ b	___ a	___ c
4	___ b	___ c	___ d	___ a
5	___ b	___ a	___ c	___ d
6	___ a	___ d	___ c	___ b
7	___ a	___ b	___ d	___ c
8	___ c	___ d	___ a	___ b
9	___ a	___ d	___ c	___ b
10	___ c	___ a	___ b	___ d
11	___ a	___ d	___ b	___ c
12	___ a	___ c	___ d	___ b
13	___ d	___ b	___ a	___ c
14	___ d	___ a	___ b	___ c
15	___ b	___ c	___ d	___ a
16	___ a	___ b	___ c	___ d
17	___ d	___ c	___ b	___ a
18	___ d	___ b	___ a	___ c
19	___ c	___ a	___ d	___ b
20	___ b	___ c	___ d	___ a

SCORING YOUR RESPONSES

Count the number of "1's" you entered in each of the Reality columns—enter those numbers in the row of the chart below labeled "1's." Then, count the number of "4's" you entered in each of the Reality columns—enter those numbers in the row of the chart below labeled "4's." Subtract the number of "4's" from the "1's" and enter the difference in the row labeled "Score." (Use negative numbers if applicable.) This is your Reality Inquiry Score. To check that you have added correctly, the total for the "1's" and "4's" rows should each equal "20." The total for the "Score" row should equal "0."

	REALITY			
	UNITARY (U)	SENSORY (SE)	SOCIAL (SO)	MYTHIC (M)
"1's"				
"4's"				
SCORE				

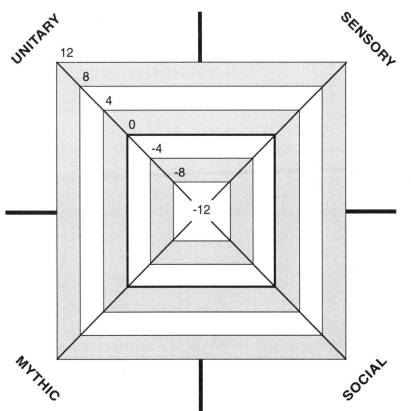

Chart the Reality Inquiry Score from the boxes above along the diagonal axes associated with each Reality, then connect those four points by lines. For example the following figure represents the score below.

U	SE	SO	M
-5	-1	2	4

Enter your Reality Inquiry
Score from the previous page
in the table to the right.

	REALITY			
	UNITARY (U)	SENSORY (SE)	SOCIAL (SO)	MYTHIC (M)
SCORE				

MODES OF CHANGE AND LEADERSHIP STYLES

From your Reality Inquiry Score you can compute your preferred Modes of Change and Leadership Styles. Add the pairs of your Reality scores in the spaces below. The addition is algebraic: For example: -2 + 3 = 1 and 4 + (-6) = -2. To check that you have added algebraically, the total for the bottom row should equal "0."

	U + SE	M + U	SO + U	SE + SO	SE + M	SO + M
MODES & STYLES	Analytic	Assertive	Influential	Evaluative	Inventive	Emergent
0 =						

PREFERRED _____

_____

_____

_____

_____

LEAST PREFERRED _____

Rank your preferences in the table to the left from the most preferred (largest positive number), to the least preferred (largest negative number). If your scores are tied, arrange them in the order that feels most familiar to you. This table lists your Modes of Change and Leadership Styles in order of preference. Modes of Change and Leadership Styles are described in detail in Chapters 2 and 3.

PATTERNS

Behavior is a product of a mixture of beliefs. While you may typically think from one world view, your responses follow from a whole configuration of beliefs—and many other factors not recognized in this model. The characterizations provided by theory are more typical and most visible in a person dominated by one belief than in a person whose beliefs are balanced, or less well defined. You can get some ideas about the behaviors that accompany your score from the following typical patterns.

DOMINANCE: A strongly one-sided score shows great focus, but also suggests little capacity to act or produce changes. For example, people who are dominantly Mythic may be creative—poets, painters, or dreamers, but are not likely to realize their ideas or get them widely accepted.

ACTIVE FOCUS: This typical pattern indicates people who use a particular style to effect change. They tend to use the same language in most of their dealing, but may vary in which direction of change they take. People with such a pattern may not overtly reject other beliefs, but they have little interest in them and must manage their lack of interest diplomatically. Here, we often see people who have strong scores in three Realities, providing an excellent base for leadership.

BALANCE: A balanced pattern seems ideal, providing freedom to work with any path and tool or to use any leadership style. However, such evenhandedness may block focused achievement. This score can also come from a random or careless completion of the instrument. Only a reading of the story can distinguish among these interpretations.

AVOIDANCE: If any score is "-8" or more minus, there is a strong indication of a rejection of that Reality. Those showing such scores are likely to experience hurt or anger in working with people displaying the rejected Reality. We commonly find such Reality patterns in people involved in change who are working against the expression of that belief. For some this is a self-rejection. In the illustrated case people might have a strong drive toward the Unitary world view but an intense anger toward that aspect of themselves. These patterns also call for a more complete interpretation based on the story and the particular score.

AND VARIATIONS... This instrument notices only two dimensions of a person's behavior. While the Realities make strong separations between different characteristic behaviors, you should not expect that two people with similar scores will be similar in every way. You may obtain a further interpretation by contacting Will McWhinney at the address given on the last page.

CHAPTER 2

The Modes of Change

THE MODES OF CHANGE

The Modes of Change are problem-solving approaches that arise from the differing ways in which we view Reality. Since each of us is proficient in a number of modes but habitually use one or another in most situations we are like the proverbial man with a hammer who finds everything to be a nail. Although we may habitually prefer one mode, by becoming proficient in the other modes we gain the freedom and power to work on any issue. The Modes of Change are designed to assist you in consciously choosing tools that make best use of your skills and available resources when working a particular problematic situation.

The different Modes of Change arise from our beliefs about Reality, change, cause, and the qualities of resolution. The modes are formed by pairings of the Unitary, Sensory, Social, and Mythic Realities. With four Realities there are six distinct pairs, and thus six Modes of Change. See the diagram to the right.

Each mode is a complete path of change, capable of forming and implementing a solution. Within each mode a solution is developed using tools of one Reality to impact a situation defined in a second. For example, the Analytical Mode operates in a world regulated by Unitary laws (physics, the law, computer programs) and realizes these in the Sensory world of facts that we see or feel (the weight of a book, evidence of a crime, graphic charts). Conversely, we may use facts about the world to test new laws or develop new procedures. Some problems are resolved within a single mode, but more often you will use a series of steps—a path—to resolve an issue. A full solution may typically use two or more modes in varied and interwoven paths.

Although people naturally tend toward one mode or another, engineers can learn to solve problems the way educators do and visa versa. The way people typically work is evidence of their preferring a particular mode; however, by becoming proficient in a variety of modes you will gain the freedom and power to work on any issue.

THE MODES OF CHANGE

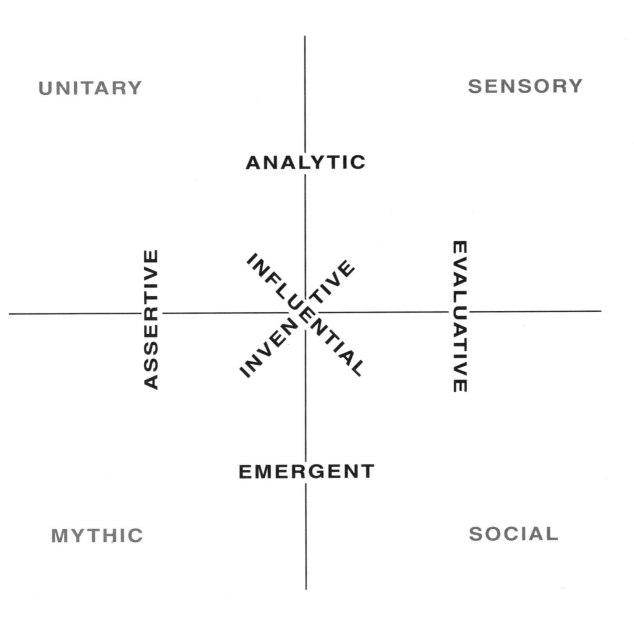

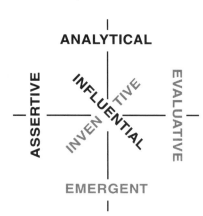

ANALYTICAL: Unitary ←→ Sensory

Thinking in the Analytical Mode often defines "rationality" for many people. Unitary theories are put into action in the Sensory world. Conversely, data is collected from the Sensory world and organized by the classifying tools of the Unitary mind. The engineer who designs fuel efficient automobiles to reduce pollution, the economic investor who purchases stocks after studying market trends, and a football player who develops strategy within the rules of the game, all solve problems in the Analytic Mode.

ASSERTIVE: Mythic ←→ Unitary

Change in the Assertive Mode is created through a charismatic leader (Mythic) or agent of authority (Unitary). These leaders develop policies that express a new vision, or create images that inspire belief in a new system. Material or intellectual propaganda is created to embody their visions. This mode is exemplified by a public relations representative creating a company image, an architect designing an avant-garde building, and a scientist who formulates a theory and asserts it to be the best explanation of facts.

INFLUENTIAL: Social ←→ Unitary

The Influential Mode gains acceptance for new values through an authority imposing a "truth" or by a population adopting a value. A social welfare minister or politician who imposes policies for the "good of the people," or an advocacy group that blocks the destruction of the environment are all working in the Influential Mode. Their focus on the issues of truth and fairness dominates their concern for facts and creative opportunities.

EVALUATIVE: Sensory ←→ Social

Change occurs in the Evaluative Mode by exploring what matters to the group (Social) based on feelings (Sensory), and finding ways to distribute values fairly. Action follows the shared acceptance of the idea. The Evaluative Mode is the mode of practical business managers, traders, and shop keepers who use their people skills to evaluate, balance, and allocate.

INVENTIVE: Sensory ←→ Mythic

A person operating in the Inventive Mode translates ideas (Mythic) into material things (Sensory), or creates ideas from data. Inventors who create machines, artists who paint, and entrepreneurs who dream up new business applications are all operating within the Inventive Mode. A purely inventive mind is little concerned with Social values or Unitary truths, only with creating ingenious and practical solutions.

EMERGENT: Social ←→ Mythic

The Emergent Mode of Change creates ideas (Mythic) that reflect values (Social) emerging from an involved group or leader. Mythic ideas gain acceptance as they reflect the Social values of a community. This is the mode of the social activist who encourages people to participate in ideas that "matter" and of the story teller who creates meaning that cultivates values.

THE DIRECTIONAL METHODS

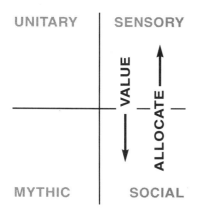

Directional Methods within the Evaluative Mode of Change

Change efforts create anew or confirm the existing situation. There are methods within each Mode of Change that direct us toward these alternatives—methods that induce new solutions and methods that put a problematic situation back together. We label these Directional Methods indicating that they work in two directions (A→B and B→A). For example, as a problem solver acting within the Evaluative Mode, you observe a gap between "what is" and "what ought to be." You can use two different approaches for the problem: you can either be motivated to clarify your *values* (Sensory→Social), or you can accept the existing values and better *allocate* your available resources (Social→Sensory). The diagram at the left charts the direction of the two problem solving alternatives, showing the two Directional Methods that *value* and *allocate* goods within the Evaluative Mode.

The *Guide to the Directional Methods* on the next pages describes all six pairs of Directional Methods within each Mode of Change. The Directional Methods name "what you are doing" at each step of the action. They identify the methods that bring about solutions or manage conflicts. As you work with the Directional Methods you may wish to refer back to the Modes of Change to refresh your ideas about the change process.

Pairs of Directional Methods are frequently used together to complete a task. In simple cases problems may be solved by using the two Directional Methods of one Mode of Change to create a simple loop. For example, in the Assertive Mode one Directional Method *establishes* a policy that expresses a vision (Mythic→Unitary), the other is *inspired* by ideas to execute a program (Unitary→Mythic).

In a simple example case, a supervisor was told to greatly reduce his workers' overtime. He chose to use the pair of Directional Methods within the Evaluative Mode (Sensory↔Social) based on a review of his situation. The supervisor began by determining what mattered to the workers. Did they prefer to work and receive pay or have more free time? He determined their preferences using the Directional Method of *valuing* (Sensory ➔ Social), with facts from the Sensory Reality to identify values in the Social Reality. Then the supervisor used the opposite Directional Method of *allocating* to "close the loop" (Social ➔ Sensory). He divided up overtime hours among workers who wanted to work overtime. He started with the workers' values (Social) and ended up with an overtime schedule (Sensory). The Tools of Change section at the back of this workbook gives details about specific tools that the supervisor might have used to *value* and *allocate*.

More complicated issues demand longer paths of resolution. You may need to use tools that carry out a series of Directional Methods to resolve an issue. Continuing the above example, the supervisor in the overtime situation determined what was *valued* by the workers (Sensory ➔ Social), but his plan did not satisfactorily *allocate* the overtime pay. He was forced to use a more extended path to find a resolution. He chose to move into the Emergent Mode, *evoking* new ideas that reflected the workers values. (Social ➔ Mythic). He reframed the problem by getting rid of overtime. Now he has used *valuing* and *evoking*, two Directional Methods from two Modes of Change, as shown in the first half of the path diagrammed at the right.

The supervisor *facilitated* (Mythic ➔ Social) designing a more efficient work routine, getting everything done within a regular eight hour day, and eliminating the need for overtime. The issue was resolved with the workers by equally *allocating* a bonus to everyone in lieu of overtime pay. Thus the group completed a loop through four Directional Methods of two modes. Choosing and working along such paths is discussed more fully in Chapter 5 of this workbook and in Chapter 5 of *The Paths of Change* (1992).

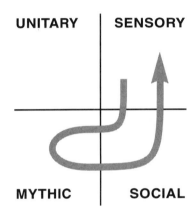

Extended Path of resolution for "overtime" example.

GUIDE   TO   THE

MODES OF CHANGE	DIRECTIONAL METHODS	BASIC ACTION	PROCESS QUESTION	PLANNING QUESTION
ANALYTIC	**DESIGN** Unitary ➙ Sensory	Put theory & policy into action.	How to apply theory & principle to a situation?	Have you built an implementation plan for introducing the design?
	TEST Sensory ➙ Unitary	Use data to interpret a situation.	What policies & theories fit a set of data?	Are you prepared to revise policies to fit the situation?
ASSERTIVE	**ESTABLISH** Mythic ➙ Unitary	Develop policies that express a vision.	How to transfer from a creative style to a structured mode of action?	What structure is needed to implement & sustain new ideas & visions?
	INSPIRE Unitary ➙ Mythic	Mobilize energy around a fresh symbol of a belief system.	What images will convey a program to others?	What will energize others to follow the new policies?
INFLUENTIAL	**PERSUADE** Social ➙ Unitary	Change policies to reflect a group's values.	How to translate values into rules & policies?	How to deal with the fear of losing their beliefs while taking on new policies?
	CONVERT Unitary ➙ Social	Convert to an established truth.	How to impose a belief system on others?	Who are the opinion leaders? What are their opposing values?

DIRECTIONAL METHODS

MODES OF CHANGE	DIRECTIONAL METHODS	BASIC ACTION	PROCESS QUESTION	PLANNING QUESTION
EVALUATIVE	VALUE Sensory → Social	Elicit what matters in a situation.	What is valued by us & others? How do we rank the values?	Who do we involve in determining a value? How do we get their views?
	ALLOCATE Social → Sensory	Allocate & assign resources & responsibilities.	What do members consider to be a fair distribution?	How to match personal abilities & desires with task requirements?
INVENTIVE	INDUCE Sensory → Mythic	Create an idea that brings clarity & meaning to a situation.	What innovative idea will reframe the problem or conflict?	What conditions will support the required creativity?
	REALIZE Mythic → Sensory	Put an idea into practice.	What form will realize an idea in time and space?	What impedes materializing the ideas & visions?
EMERGENT	EVOKE Social → Mythic	Co-create ideas or images that reflect values.	What ideas & images symbolize what matters to us?	What conditions must be set up to find new symbols for our values?
	FACILITATE Mythic → Social	Get others to value an idea.	How do we gain acceptance of an idea?	What framing of the situation will gain acceptance from others?

CHAPTER 3

Leadership and the Team

WHAT IS YOUR LEADERSHIP STYLE?

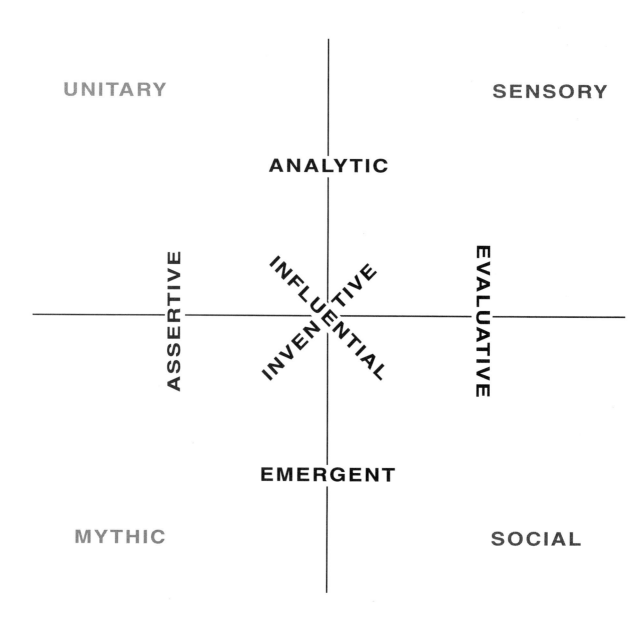

ANALYTICAL: Unitary ◄──► Sensory

Uses data and principles (theory and policy) to make decisions.

Plans the use of resources and tests the effectiveness of the work.

ASSERTIVE: Mythic ◄──► Unitary

Creates and propagates symbols, images, and ideals which

give direction to a group or community.

INFLUENTIAL: Social ◄──► Unitary

Listens to and incorporates a group's ideas and preferences as

suggestions for carrying out the organization's goals.

EVALUATIVE: Sensory ◄──► Social

Works with people, incorporating their ideas, values, and pref-

erences into the solution.

INVENTIVE: Sensory ◄──► Mythic

Makes new ideas happen.

EMERGENT: Social ◄──► Mythic

Supports a group and its leaders to find solutions: sometimes

as guide through the process, other times as a contributing

member.

THE REALITIES OF LEADING

"Being a good leader depends on how well you match your Leadership Style, energy, and other personal attributes with your co-workers and the presenting problem."

Just as the Modes of Change follow from the Reality preferences, so do the natural *Leadership Styles*. Being an effective leader depends on how well you match your style, energy, and other personal attributes with your co-workers and the presenting problem. Similarly, the performance of a group or organization depends on the dominant realities of its group members, and the problematic situation. Here we introduce characteristics of the Leadership Styles, and the dynamics of team members among the various realities.

Change is dependent upon using the tools of one Reality to make an impact on something defined in a second Reality. Thus, effective leadership requires that a leader have skills defined in at least two realities. People who are in the habit of seeing a single Reality are not likely to be effective in either change or leadership. The Unitary person will follow "the system;" the Sensory will reflect on perception; the Social will lock into unending explorations of feelings; and the Mythic will dance with dreams.

We define a Leadership Style in terms of a person's typical choice when using one of the six pairs of Realities to achieve changes. These six basic styles are described in the *Leadership Styles* chart to the right. For example, Analytic leaders focus on the immediate task, using the available technologies to achieve policy goals (Unitary ◄──► Sensory). Evaluative leaders assign and manage tasks based on their preferences or those of the work group (Social ◄──► Sensory). Assertive leaders give direction to a group using popular images, old heroes, and honored truths (Mythic ◄──► Unitary).

Leadership Styles are expressed in the way leaders typically work with colleagues, subordinates, and stakeholders in the environment of the situation. Some leaders effectively use a single style most of the time, while others may choose between two or more styles depending upon the situation. In the United States today the ideal image of a corporate executive is a person who is

LEADERSHIP STYLES

	LEADERSHIP ROLE & FOCUS	ORGANIZING STYLE	PLANNING STYLE	DEALING WITH CONFLICT
ANALYTIC U ⟷ SE	Logically exercising power to achieve established goals.	Task hierarchical, meritocracy.	Explicit responsibility, time & resource assignments.	Referee disputes and move on.
ASSERTIVE M ⟷ U	Establish a mission, with authority; exhort loyalty to the person and mission of the leader.	Tribal, sacred, charismatic, evolving toward bureaucracy.	Autocratic, big picture, with a long view.	Establish authoritarian solution or creatively reframe the issue.
INFLUENTIAL U ⟷ SO	Work politically to effect the optimal policies to attain organizational goals.	Patriarchal or oligarchic; strong committee structure.	Maintaining, or radically reforming, the game; protecting the reigning power-value balance.	Negotiate & mediate disputes to group the power base around established & valued positions.
EVALUATIVE SE ⟷ SO	Properly allocate human & physical resources for short & long term outcomes.	Functionally responsive to wishes of participants.	Optimizing (equalizing) assignment of work and benefits over time.	Negotiate for win-win values.
INVENTIVE M ⟷ SE	Materialize one's personal ideas in the real world.	Charismatic, evolving toward task hierarchy.	Highly flexible, but with strong achievement drive.	Wipe out power base of opposition. Reemphasize group goal to subordinate dispute.
EMERGENT SO ⟷ M	Co-create valued images with the energy & skills of participants.	Open flexible functionality; socially supportive.	Expansive, search oriented efforts to take advantage of opportunities.	Exploration for possible solutions; creatively reframe rather than solve.

entrepreneurial (Inventive), provides new meaning (Emergent), and manages well (Evaluative). A combination of Assertive and Emergent leadership styles work particularly well within religious leadership. The ultimate leader has access to all leadership styles and has the wisdom to know when to employ each.

Most of the activities that are popularly called "leadership" might better be termed managing, supervising, innovating, facilitating, etc. The concept of leadership takes on a very different role within the setting of each Reality. There is no general activity called "leading." Only the Mythic person can make meaning; the Unitary speaks from authority; the Sensory sees from the objective world; and the Social determines what matters. Leadership functions are specific to the dominant Reality. Leadership effectiveness is also determined by the situation. A leader who would maintain an organization acts differently from one who will change it. The maintainer weaves over conflict; the changer induces conflict. Some writers would prefer to limit the term "leadership" to the Emergent function of creating meaning within a group or community. While this style may be the epitome of leadership, we maintain the broader use of this term, applying it to the various styles one would use to achieve change.

YOUR LEADERSHIP STYLE

Review your "Mode and Styles Score" on page 26 of the *Reality Inquiry*. The Inquiry provides a reliable indicator of your preferred Leadership Styles. Does the score in the Reality Inquiry fit your self-image? Does it suggest that you focus on a particular style, or does it support an impression that you easily work with others in a variety of ways?

A dominant score in any of the six modes signifies a strongly formed style. For example, if you show a dominant Evaluative Mode you will likely *evaluate* what is important and *allocate* resources accordingly—a style that has long been popular in American management.

If your score is strongly dominated by one of the four Realities, you may fixate on that Reality and lack a developed

Leadership Style. Remember, change and leadership are both dependent upon having skills in two Realities. For example, if you have a strongly dominant Social Reality you may concentrate only on values and feelings within the group, hesitating to make the decisions required of a leader.

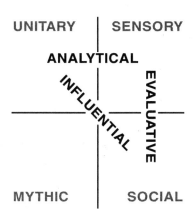

Strong scores on three Realities indicate that you can use any set of associated styles. A balanced "Unitary–Sensory–Social" score indicates you could use Analytic, Evaluative, and Influential Leadership Styles over the course of your work. However, you may have training in a technical subject such as engineering, finance, or law, and be more comfortable using the Analytic style than one calling for the interpretation of emotions.

Balanced scores in the Unitary, Sensory, and Social Realities.

A score showing no marked preference may indicate that you are capable of using any style. This can give you great freedom to work in a variety of situations. Alternatively, it may suggest you have not developed clearly differentiated actions or Leadership Styles. To decide which applies to you look at your work history and talk with co-workers. You may also contact Will McWhinney to clarify what your Reality Inquiry writing indicates.

Your effectiveness as a leader, manager, mentor, administrator, or consultant partially depends on the group within which you are creating change. If you limit yourself to a single Leadership Style, you are likely to be effective only with groups of people whose dominant styles condition them to work with your style.

LEADERS AND TEAM MEMBERS

The performance of a group or organization is dependent upon the Realities of its leaders and team members, as well as the environment upon which they are making an impact. Leaders seldom solve problems within an organization, family, or community by themselves. They work with other people as colleagues, team members, fellow participants, and followers. Usually leaders and team members work together to clarify thinking, develop ideas, and gain confidence in existing beliefs. Your success as a leader depends not only on your personal skills, but also on your ability to assemble a team, identifying people who will follow you, be empowered by you, or accept your authority.

In some circumstances a job will only require momentary help from others: offering information, authorizing an action, or listening as a leader thinks aloud. The association is momentary and matching personal styles is of little importance. Sometimes your interaction will be limited to the task, but more frequently you will work with groups or individuals over extended periods of time and in various roles. The effectiveness of such relations, and the joy you get from them, depends upon how well your world views complement each other. For example, two people of dominantly Social views may get along splendidly. A Sensory and a Social may have less to talk about but complete the task more quickly. Your interaction with the team members and the effectiveness of each member will vary over the course of work. Along a path of resolution you may need different mixes of Reality views to produce the desired outcomes.

BUILDING AN EFFECTIVE TEAM

When forming a problem-solving team it is essential to consider the mixture of Realities the group needs in order to get the task done. What problem-solving approach seems most effective for the situation? Can team members use this problem-solving approach? How will team members work together? Successful leaders must consciously develop a team with world views appropriate to the presenting task. Leaders must blend their own Leadership Style and the Realities of the group to effectively build a Path of Change.

There is a strong tendency for people with similar world views to congregate in groups. For example: people who work in organizational development and training tend to be of a dominantly Social Reality. Information system designers and accountants usually hold a Unitary Reality. Engineers are more likely to have a strong Sensory Reality. Because of a commitment to a common world view, people of like Realities are more comfortable working together. People naturally slip into working with groups that share a single world view. Unfortunately, teams consisting of one dominant world view are usually not likely to engage in change and are often ineffective at problem solving. We must confront the issues of mixing world views to facilitate the use of all the required Modes of Change.

For a particular task you may need a team with special abilities: people with Sensory Realities to do a survey of a population, or people with Mythic ◄──► Unitary habits to create an advertising campaign. Alternatively, you may wish to develop a work group with team members from all Realities. A balanced group with advocates from all Realities may allow you to work on a variety of issues, but will likely face conflict in every effort to solve problems. The solutions put forward from such groups are likely to be compromises. A group that works from a focused Reality may produce stronger and clearer actions.

Without conscious selection you are not likely to have the Reality bases covered that the work will require. For example, take an insurance company that wants to expand into a new line of loans that are far riskier than their present business ventures. The company finds that none of their current executives exhibit a strong Assertive Leadership Style. Lacking the appropriate risk-taking leader for the task, the company delays the expansion until an Assertive leader is found. Another type of problem arises when a leader inherits a team assembled by another leader for the purpose of solving a problem different from the immediate task. The leader is then faced with developing confluence among team members rather than selecting members on the basis of task requirements.

When building teams, leaders must examine how people of differing dominant Realities work together. The *Leaders and Team Members* chart, on the following page, gives information about the probable relations between leaders and team members with varying Reality preferences. To use the chart you need to estimate both the leader's and team members' dominant Realities.

LEADERS AND TEAM MEMBERS

		LEADER'S REALITY			
		UNITARY	**SENSORY**	**SOCIAL**	**MYTHIC**
MEMBER'S REALITY	**UNITARY**	**FOLLOWER** Experiences certitude unless followers fear that the leader holds heretical beliefs.	Unconstructive Little respect for leader, ignores and passively blocks most change efforts.	Unconstructive Disrespect unless they share common values; threatened by social values.	**FOLLOWER** Strongly supports Charismatic leader, but strongly opposes if leader calls for radical changes.
	SENSORY	Acquiescent Accepts power & rules as long as they work.	**COLLEAGUE** Authority given to expertise rather than to the person.	Unconstructive Low regard for leader, ignores ideas & values.	**INDEPENDENT** Uncommitted, but will use any opportunities provided.
	SOCIAL	Reactive Usually counters leadership: reactive, negative.	Unwilling Follower Low regard. Today the Social often goes along while educating the leader.	**TEAM MEMBER** Trust, cooperation, good communication.	Involved Opposes, unless the leader is strongly facilitative, then a strong supporter.
	MYTHIC	User Uses leader even as a subordinate, as a channel to power or a front for follower's operations.	**INDEPENDENT** Uses resources to accomplish own aim. Mythic is likely to respect a strong Sensory leader.	User Uses the leader as a support for own development.	Learner Will not follow, but learns from leader often in strong love/hate dilemma.

*Responses printed in **BOLD** indicate particularly **constructive** forms of relating between leaders and team members according to their dominant Reality styles. The other relations are less likely to fully support the leader's efforts or the team members' personal development. This table indicates the responses of pure Reality types. The actual behavior of team members will be some mixture of archetypal behaviors.*

A Sample Reading of This Chart

FROM THE LEADER'S PERSPECTIVE:

As a leader, the individuals in your group will respond to you differently according to the match of Realities. Understanding the varying quality of relations will assist you when assembling a team or working with an existing team. For example, if your dominant Reality is strongly Social, other Socials are most likely to respond constructively to your leadership. If you have a strong Sensory component as well, you may find colleagues among some Sensory and Mythic types.

If you are dominantly a Mythic leader, you may be attracted to having creative energetic people such as yourself work for you. However, after a short internship they are likely to become competitive and induce destructive contests for leadership of ideas and for followers. In this situation, Sensories on the team will be annoyed by the conflict, thinking it interferes with getting things done. The Unitaries are likely to be the most or least useful to a Mythic leader—most, because they carry out orders; least, because they insist on orderliness over effectiveness. Achieving cooperation is difficult with some collections of differing world views. However, a strong leader can overcome stylistic preferences regardless of the team member's dominant world views.

FROM THE TEAM MEMBER'S PERSPECTIVE:

As a team member, the leader's relations with you are similarly dependent on your respective Realities. For example, if you have a dominant Unitary Reality, you are likely to find working with either Sensory or Social leaders to be stressful. If you are a Mythic, you should recognize that leaders are likely to see you as creative and energetic but not reliable; if you are to remain effective within a work group, you need to manage your energy.

Selecting mentors also requires careful matching to assure that their guidance is proper for your style. For example, an exciting and successful Mythic may be an energizing model, but not be a responsive mentor. However, a Sensory mentor may not encourage the weak follower but is valuable to contain a Mythic's exuberance.

Perhaps the most controllable source of failure within an organizational change effort is dysfunctional activity within the change team itself. This is as true for an organizational development team as it is for a political campaign or an urban renewal project. Without conscious work most relationships in organizations are at best unconstructive. Knowing this natural outcome aids you in transcending the difficulties that arise from habitual behaviors.

Constructive interrelations and mutual support among team members are critical to success of any work. You may wish to gain strength by having a divergent set of people on the team; however, managing a team becomes increasingly difficult when members have varied Reality preferences. Even though it contributes to the overall ability of a group, mixes of dominant Realities of the leader and team members can introduce unpredictable behavior.

The blend of Realities within a team leads to different courses of direction, sometimes toward effective group behavior and sometimes locking the group into restrictive "norms," resulting in ineffective performance. Restrictive norming is likely to occur in diverse groups when the results of a team's efforts are unclear and rewards and punishments do not closely match performance. Without good feedback a group will turn inward and begin to respond superstitiously to task issues, blocking any behavior that deviates from the norm.

Norming is particularly destructive behavior in professional and craft groups. There it is more likely to be reinforced since people within an established field will likely habitually drive out others with deviating world views. Norming is even seen in highly creative organizations that gradually turn inward and lose contact with their stakeholders. Apple Computers is a highly visible example in which the normalized behavior of computer professionals wiped out its market advantages. The trouble often begins when forming the team. A team is more likely to retain its effective behavior if the members join the group as whole people, not just as "hands," "eyes," or a "brain" hired to do a specific task. People are naturally multiskilled, curious, and open. They stop learning if fear and interpersonal conflict tend to eliminate trust and direction.

To stay open to achievement a group must continually share task and personal information among group members as well as with outside sources.

YOUR TEAM PROFILE

A critical step in team building is getting a sense of the distribution of Realities within the group. Ideally everyone would take the Reality Inquiry, discuss the mixture of Realities, explore the potential opportunities, and identify danger points as an early step in developing the confluence of the team. Even without Reality scores, you can apply the concepts from the first few chapters and approximate the distribution of the team's dominant Realities. With a shared appreciation of each others' world views, you can collectively choose how you will work each task confronting you.

Completing the Reality Matrix on the following pages provides a map of your team, identifying potential strengths and weaknesses. First focus on the team members' abilities to work together and resolve issues that arise within the team. Such consideration may lead to the team taking time to develop the necessary confluence of purpose, skills, attitudes, and mutual knowledge. Secondly, have team members consider the environment in which the problem is located. What are the Leadership Styles of the existing authority figures? What are the dominant Realities of the organizations your team encounters?

Finally, your team should consider the demands of the environment. The positioning of members must be designed to match the configuration of forces (dominant Realities) in the environment. With a shared appreciation of each others' Realities you can collectively choose appropriate Leadership Styles and develop Paths of Change. Remember that people of like Realities tend to congregate and accentuate their similarities. Consequently, your team may be more focused on one Reality than the results of the individual Reality scores indicate. Complete the Reality Matrix on the following pages to clarify the information you have gathered about yourself, your co-workers, and the environment of the issue.

FILLING OUT THE REALITY MATRIX

Use the following questions to fill out the Reality Matrix on the following page. The questions will aid you when selecting the best Modes and Paths of Change for your problematic situation.

1. Please enter your dominant Mode of Change: _____

    Are you most comfortable using this mode?
    If not, note the mode you prefer using: _____

    Note the mode most typically used by the for-
    mal leader of the effort, if this is not your role: _____

2. Note the team's preferred Modes of Change: _____

3. Note which of the four Realities are dominant
    among people who will ultimately authorize or
    block changes in the Environment of the issue: _____

**NOTE: SEE PAGE 96 FOR A COMPLETED
EXAMPLE OF THE REALITY MATRIX.**

THE REALITY MATRIX

UNITARY	SENSORY
MYTHIC	SOCIAL

WHEN FILLING OUT THE MATRIX:

*Draw a line that represents **Your dominant Mode** (or Modes) from your Reality Inquiry score:*

*Draw an oval that encompasses the concentration of the **Team's preferred Modes:***

*Shade the quadrants that represent the dominant **Realities** of the people in the **Environment** who will authorize or block changes:*

CHAPTER 4

The Games of Change

"What games do we play in the real world?"

> "They're not games like checkers or chess.
> They're much more complicated than those sorts of games."

"How can they be more complicated than chess? That's a game of experts"

> "Well, the rules aren't set. People make them up as they go along
> and fight with others who don't want to change. These are the
> games of *leaders* and *politicians*."

"If they make up rules I don't like, I won't play."

> "You've just entered another game. It is called *economics*, choosing
> how to use your time and energy."

"O.K., then I'll create my own games and convince others to play with me."

> "Those are just more games. The games of *invention*, and of building
> friendship and tradition by creating *culture*."

THE GAMES OF CHANGE

We all know the language of the games people play. "Are you game for that?" "What are the rules?" "We're not in their league." "The games of love and war." Gaming is a metaphor through which we characterize the way we engage with others to bring about change. We introduce the game metaphor here to clarify how each Mode of Change is used in everyday problem solving. Each of the six Mode of Change is characterized by a different *Game of Change.*

The six Games of Change have different rules, stakes, customs, and environments. The games attract people of different personal styles. We label these games according to the kinds of boards on which they are played—a chess board, a boardroom table, an architect's drawing board, or the street where you live. We identify six Boards of Change—one for each of the six Games of Change. On four of the boards the games are adversarial, with winners and losers. On the other two, the play is collaborative.

The play on each board serves a different role in society. We need to respect the various boards if we are to be successful in our change efforts. We need to know on which boards everyone is playing. Scientists play by rigid rules testing hypotheses, constructing detailed reports, and facing scrutiny. Politicians bend the rules, trying to create a game that favors their constituencies. The supply and demand of the marketplace involves other games. We also play the games of love and learning, sometimes competitively, sometimes cooperatively. Lovers and scientists get hurt if they do not recognize that they are playing with politicians. We all lose when we reduce the game of creating meaning to the cut throat policies of the economic marketplace. Learning to play on the appropriate boards is *The Game of Change.*

"Games are consciously or implicitly played all the time. Expertise, power, value, and meaning are constant issues in our lives."

Learning to play on the appropriate boards is The Game of Change.

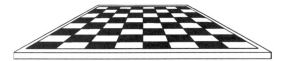

THE MASTER GAMES OF CHANGE

	MODES OF CHANGE	BOARD	GAME	GOALS	PLAY	ACTIVITIES
COMPETITIVE GAMES	ANALYTIC	1ST	**SAME GAME**	Play most competently within the rules	Expert Action	Choosing the moves on the visible board
	ASSERTIVE	2ND	**NEW RULES**	Gain advantage (power) for play on the First Board	Set Policy	Taking charge of the rules and maintaining order
	INFLUENTIAL	3RD	**NEW VALUES**	Set values for ethical play	Work the value bases of policy	Working ethical & human relations issues
	EVALUATIVE	4TH	**MARKET-PLACE**	Motivate involved parties to effectively use resources	Assign values & rewards	Communicating, bargaining, & allocating
COLLABORATIVE GAMES	INVENTIVE	5TH	**NEW GAMES**	Create new games; make novel things work	Explore opportunities; Entrepreneur	Playing with play
	EMERGENT	6TH	**NEW CULTURE**	Enhancing spirit, meaning & opportunities	Display vision & meaning	Creating the culture of play

Note: Expanded from an earlier version with contributions by Tamara Bliss

THE SIX GAMES OF CHANGE

The **FIRST** game is played on a well defined board, such as the board of chess and checkers. Rules and clear objectives define a game of skill, clearly separating winners from losers. The skilled player is a technologist who excels by *analyzing* the rules of the game, and applying them within the tangible world.

The **SECOND** game is played on a variety of boards, "The Board of Directors," "The Board of Trade," and "The Board of Review." Members *assert* and establish new rules which the players will use on the First Board. The moves on the Second Board create advantages on the First Board of skill.

The **THIRD** game and the board on which it is played are less tangible. Players strive to *influence* policies and social values. Both sides can be within an organization, e.g., industrial relations managers versus production supervisors. Or, opponents can be outside the organization, e.g., customers, regulators, advocacy groups, and political adversaries. The game is won by making, modifying, or reestablishing values which underlie the organization's policies. These changes appear as different policies and objectives for players of the First Board.

The **FOURTH** Board is the marketplace—it is the game of communication and commerce. It operates by *evaluating* worth in exchange for rewards, e.g., goods for services, effort for money, and time for opportunities. The players may be adversarial on the market or cooperative in communication.

The **FIFTH** game transcends limitations set by the game board metaphor by *inventing* new games. Play gives birth to new products, opportunities, and organizations. Present games and rules of play are reshaped, creating radically new enterprises. Players on the Fifth Board are focused on the experience of play. The game is won by creating new products for the market or even creating new markets. The intent of play is collaborative; however, new games can compete with established ones, rendering the skills of experts on other boards useless.

The **SIXTH** Board is also a collaborative effort, and not a formal game; there are no opposing sides. New Social meanings, patterns of interaction, and ways of living *emerge* from play. The Sixth Board exceeds inventions of the Fifth by changing Social values: using mediation instead of the law courts, communicating via the Internet, and "rap" music as a new political media. Play here indicates widespread change and vitality of a whole community; however, it can also devalue cultural capital in the creation of new symbolic meanings.

THE GAME OF PROFESSIONAL BASKETBALL

Games are consciously or implicitly played all the time. Expertise, power, value, and meaning are constant issues in our lives. Leaders and team members specialize in games where they can play most successfully. This is evident in sport and business, politics and art, ethics and religion. The game of professional basketball can be used to illustrate one institution's play on all six Boards of Change.

Basketball as a game of skill is played on the **First Board**. Players adhere to the **same game** rules, develop strategies for successful play, and know what constitutes a win. Rules and expertise determine the play and who wins.

Games on the **Second Board** create **new rules** for playing basketball. Coaches, team members, managers, and occasionally a sports writer or publicist develop new ways to play outside the rules, hoping to shift the advantage in their favor. This is the game of power, persuasion, influence, and assertion. The end play occurs at a conference table where proposals are either accepted or blocked. Timing is critical to gaining acceptance, and also affects the possibility of momentary advantage while others settle into the new rules and policies. Winners on the Second Board are usually determined by the politics of the Third Board.

Play on the **Third Board** creates **new values** within the game of basketball. The pursuit of favorable public opinion is used to create power for a team, e.g., a basketball player's image, tales of good sportsmanship, banquet speeches honoring retiring coaches, and the community spirit that follows a winning team. The envelope of fair play is extended to include anything that makes basketball more appealing to players, spectators, and investors. Anyone can play on the Third Board and the rules are not well defined. Players are likely to push the rules, playing games that are unauthorized but remain within established ethical boundaries. Overt conflict is most likely to occur on this board, because it calls for change within the belief systems of rules and values that are particularly resistant to change. Winning players conduct a balancing act between tilting the table to their advantage, and remaining within the boundaries of good sportsmanship.

Play on the **Fourth Board** is a competition against forces outside the game of basketball. Here the basketball leagues compete with home videos, golf, hockey, and theme parks. Leagues hope to profit in the **marketplace** by evaluating and allocating their resources properly: selling tickets, acquiring players, bargaining with communities for a forum, and selling the show to TV networks. The players on this board compete for contracts, money, time, and attention. It resembles the First Board in that rules are fairly clear, contracts are between identified parties, penalties for contract violations are established in the law courts, and winning is measured by the exchanges of money. The required skills center around evaluating and allocating, versus the skill and expertise of the First Board. Winners close deals and gain rewards within the marketplace.

Basketball was invented, as are all **new games**, on the **Fifth Board**. Here it was conceived, given a name, and made meaningful to the sporting world. On the Fifth Board the game *is* play. The Fifth Board does not determine who will play, what the rules will be, or the expected gains. Basketball was invented over a hundred years ago, but lesser inventions continue to emerge and are applied as moves on the other boards. Inventive tactics such as an "alley-oop" (intentionally deflecting a high pass into the basket) and the "fast break" strategy appear as skill on the First Board. Development of the "three-point basket," an invention on the Fifth Board, appears as a new rule on the Second. New games are created on the Fifth Board to enhance play; there is no concept of losing.

The leadership of great players creates career paths out of poverty for young minority athletes; this is the **new culture** of the **Sixth Board** play. It is a game that creates meaning and opportunities. On the Sixth Board, the whole institution of basketball wins or loses by how it supports other institutions in society, other sports, media, entertainment, individual recreation, and the development of its players and staff. Success is the creation of meaning, visible in instances such as the impact an established professional franchise has on a city. Everyone wins here; the resulting squabbles are resolved on lower numbered boards.

In reading the description of basketball's many games, you may notice what attracts you or bothers you about play on the various boards. Each of us has preferred forms of play and will perceive play to occur on different boards. If a basketball team is winning, one person will see the quality of the team's fundamentals of play; another will see the influence of a smart manager; another will praise the style of play; and a fourth will think up a new video replay gimmick to involve the audience. This principle is the same in the work place. Some of us believe we solve problems by building an employee's skills, some by redesigning the work, others by changing the motivation, and still others by innovation in marketing of the goods. Each of us has a favorite board on which to play, where we utilize our best skills. Complex issue resolution within society and business requires the consideration of all boards. Knowledge of how and when to use each board will allow productive play and competition in many arenas.

SOME IMPLICATIONS OF PLAY

In addition to identifying the fundamentals of the six games, you need to learn when it is advantageous to play on each board. Understanding yourself as the change agent, learning the methods for making changes, and knowing the processes of leading and following will aid you in knowing when to play on each board.

The most fundamental understanding for selecting boards of play is that boards are organized into a hierarchy of dominance. The order of dominance is not necessarily fixed and may vary depending upon the environment. For example, priorities are not likely to be the same within a religious society, the United Nations, NASA, or at a marital counseling session. Consequently, the hierarchy of dominance will vary. The hierarchy employed here is a structural order specific to the thinking of our society and culture. Generally, the higher numbered boards provide a broader and deeper range of solutions, and thus more opportunities for achieving long term resolutions. However, it is not necessary to rebuild an entire house to fix a leaky roof; and play on every board has an essential role.

Play on a lower game board is restricted by play on the higher boards. Solutions to problems on any given board are generally designed within the restrictions of the game "above it." No matter how skillfully you play you can not win games by violating the rules, nor can you retain productive executives if you under pay them. Violations of this restriction are typically destructive.

Conflicts on lower boards can be dissolved by plays on higher boards. The freedom and perspective available on a higher board often resolves an apparent problem on a lower board. For example, an automotive part may cost too much per unit to manufacture; however, the invention of a new and cheaper material may solve this problem. This is Einstein's rule that we can not solve problems at the same level on which they were posed.

Play on one board gives us little guidance as to how to play on other boards. Skill in playing on the soccer field is not helpful when debating a rule with a referee; nor will skills in marketing replace hours of shooting baskets.

Some people sense that, for them, play on some boards is taboo! Only more powerful or more approved people are allowed in those games. These taboos are residues of old prejudices made visible through the game boards. Workers are not typically "supposed" to talk about corporate policy or point out the unethical behavior of superiors.

Few people enjoy playing on more than one board at a time. Trying to resolve problems against more than one set of goals at a time produces additional dilemmas, and unresolvable tensions. It is better explicitly to shift back and forth, working to attain one type of goal, then the other. Goals within an effort can be divided up so individuals play on their preferred boards. The team then shifts from one board to another, using the team members' strengths on their preferred boards to achieve goals. Solving the goals consecutively gives the appearance that the team is able to work across multiple boards. The flexibility to work on multiple boards calls for people with skills on various boards.

Switching boards without announcing the change to other players produces conflict. Switching boards adds goal conflicts to whatever other problems are already on the table. When you sense a switching of boards, it is appropriate to stop the play and negotiate the change. When discussing a university budget, an administrator who focuses on budget reduction is playing on a different board than one arguing the merits of affirmative action.

USING THE BOARDS

The sense of play on the boards makes us aware of differing customs and traditions of various groups in our society. Managers typically live in a different world of action than public relations officers or scientists. Each Mode of Change evolves in a different context that has a complete culture of its own. Traveling a Path of Change will lead you and your organization through these different cultures and require you to respond empathetically.

Following a Path of Change is more like international travel than we might wish. Envision the changes necessary for a basketball player to move to the position of umpire, manager, owner, or sports broadcaster. The varying positions call for different clothes, vocabulary, and decision styles—all the qualities that follow from maintaining different views of Reality. When solving problems, you need to pause before entering a new culture. You must examine the group, its values, structures, and the tempo of its play and adjust your style accordingly.

CHAPTER 5

The Paths of Change

THE PATHS OF CHANGE

"Paths of Change can be both simple and complex, whatever it takes to get the job done."

"A skillfully designed Path of Change allows you to resolve a series of problems that arise within the process of solving the larger issue."

A *Path of Change* is a sequence of steps to resolving a problem. A path includes two or more of the Directional Methods introduced in Chapter 2, *The Modes of Change*. As an initiator of the path you identify the presenting problem, assess your resources, scan the relevant issues in the environment, and then develop a path toward resolution. You need to take a strategic look ahead to determine both the desired outcomes and the steps to take toward resolution. Following a Path of Change may call on a variety of Leadership Styles and Modes of Change. When designing a path, you must reflect on your ability to operate within the culture of each chosen Board. As the initiator, you need to support your team members in transcending the limitations of their habitual styles, and bring insights into the culture of the problematic situation.

Paths of Change can be both simple and complex, whatever it takes to get the job done. Sometimes analysis of a problem leads you toward a simple solution. The problem can be resolved by using both Directional Methods within a Mode of Change. For example, solving a problem using the Directional Methods within the Evaluative Mode would *allocate* (Sensory → Social) resources depending upon their determined *value* (Social → Sensory). More frequently, your problem solving assessment will reveal the need for work within multiple Modes of Change, and thus require a multi-step path to resolve the problem. For example, an idea might be developed to *induce* action (Inventive Mode, Sensory → Mythic), a policy would be *established* (Assertive Mode, Mythic → Unitary), then *designed* and put into action (Analytic Mode, Unitary → Sensory).

A skillfully designed Path of Change allows you to resolve a series of problems that arise within the process of solving the larger issue. Later in this chapter, we present summaries of some minor paths and two Grand Paths of Change, Revitalization and Renaissance. A Revitalization path strengthens an organization. A Renaissance path creates a new organization through rebirth.

INITIATING A PATH OF CHANGE

From a starting point in any of the four Realities there are three ways to initiate change and solve a problem. For example, the diagram to the right shows that from the Sensory Reality you have three choices on your path toward resolution: Sensory → Unitary, forming policies along a Revitalizing route; Sensory → Social, inquiring about values along a Renaissance path; or Sensory → Mythic, forming a new idea in a creative effort. From each starting point there is a different trio of opportunities.

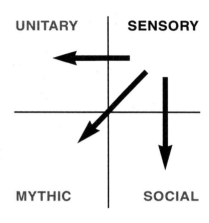

We usually start working a problem where we observe it in the Sensory Reality. This is the Reality of the physical world, where we experience pain and disappointment that leads us to change. Data is collected, facts identified, and action initiated. Sometimes, you may be given a problem to solve that appears in another Reality. For example, a superior tells you to create a brochure that reflects company image and values. This task falls within the Sixth Board of Change, the Emergent Mode (Social → Mythic). In such a case, your involvement with the problem occurs part way through a Path of Change, long after the initial Sensory awareness of a difficulty. Your superior already made the decision to take action, and your involvement is part of an ongoing path.

Although many combinations of the methods are used to follow a Path of Change, the final problem solving action leads you back into the Sensory Reality. Since problems are usually solved by actions, this is a logical place end. For example, on the First Board everyone is playing by the *same rules*; the Analytic Mode designs a solution for implementation (Unitary → Sensory). The Fourth Board is the *marketplace*; the Evaluative Mode allocates tangible resources and responsibilities (Social → Sensory). And once in a while, the Inventive Mode of the Fifth Board is used to *realize* an idea and put it directly into practice (Mythic → Sensory). All of these Directional Methods result in action, which is necessary to produce change and solve conflicts.

THE REVITALIZATION PATH

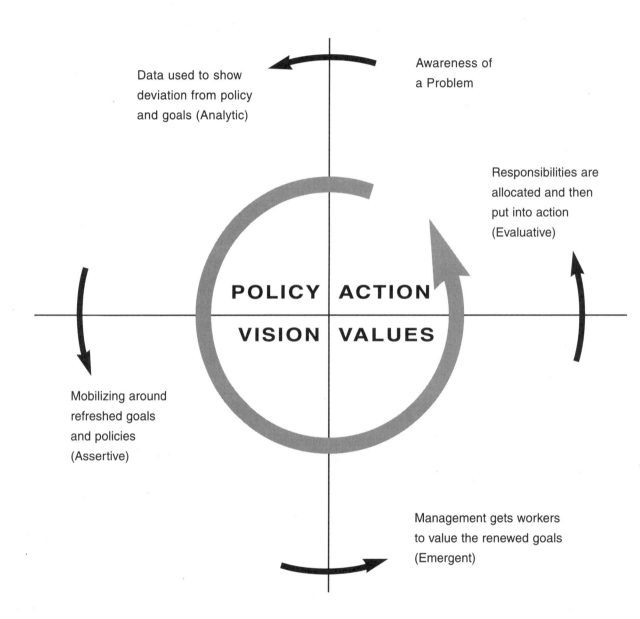

Awareness of
a Problem

Data used to show
deviation from policy
and goals (Analytic)

Responsibilities are
allocated and then
put into action
(Evaluative)

POLICY | ACTION

VISION | VALUES

Mobilizing around
refreshed goals
and policies
(Assertive)

Management gets workers
to value the renewed goals
(Emergent)

THE RENAISSANCE PATH

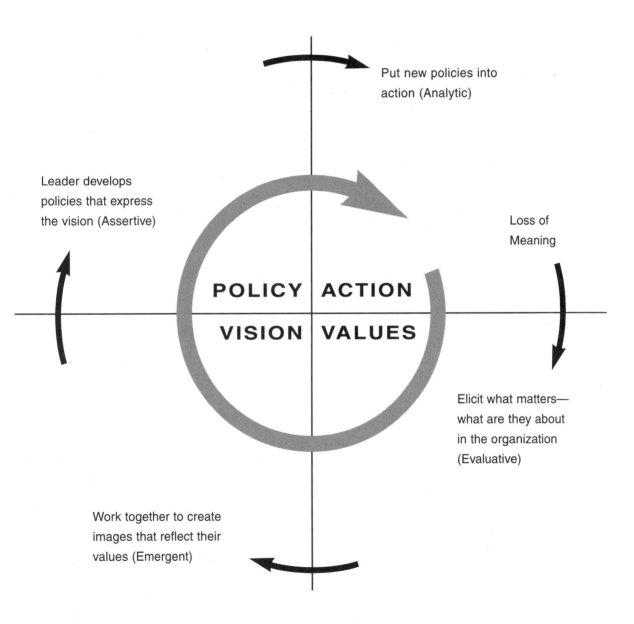

Put new policies into
action (Analytic)

Leader develops
policies that express
the vision (Assertive)

Loss of
Meaning

POLICY | ACTION
VISION | VALUES

Elicit what matters—
what are they about
in the organization
(Evaluative)

Work together to create
images that reflect their
values (Emergent)

TWO GRAND PATHS OF CHANGE

The two Grand Paths of Change follow circular routes starting and ending in the Sensory Reality. We have named these in accord with their long histories: the Revitalization path that strengthens an organization, and the Renaissance path through which ailing organizations are reborn in new forms. Each calls for problem-solving skills and Leadership Styles of all the Realities. Choosing to follow either path is a grand act of leadership. What we describe here are pure cases. In practice, you will use mixed strategies, looping back along the paths and making wide detours.

Of the two Grand Paths, the path of Revitalization is used more frequently. It is used for cleaning up a situation, doing something more efficiently, or using a new technique to tackle old problems. It supports the existing organizational capital, the livelihood, and meaning for those who have been long associated with the organization. It is the path of adaptation in response to moderate crises.

The Renaissance path is the classic path of desperation and opportunity—the path of an organization or community that has lost its sense of direction or relevance to its environment. Renaissance is called for when organizations or communities face conflicts that threaten their existence: the leadership is failing, a dominant product line is made obsolete, or the supporting social values fade. The availability of attractive alternatives rupture the established boundaries, setting conditions for breaking old allegiances to find new purposes, new membership, and new resources. The breakup of AT&T in the 1980's is a classic example of Renaissance. The breakup was followed by emergence of the several Baby Bells as new free-standing organizations. The USSR followed that path a few years later. It also happens on a micro level every day, e.g., divorces, business failures, and the restructuring that occurs when a leader dies.

The Renaissance path is increasingly used for innovation, and for creating new organizations. At one time, a single entrepreneur would have started a new business. Today, a new project will usually begin with a group thoughtfully scanning the markets, developing a team, and consciously building a culture and the new vision. These could be free standing startups, or new projects within a company. General Motors used this process to start up the Saturn project. Many companies have set up new factories in "green fields" to allow such new foundings to be free of the constraints and values of the existing organization. Renaissance, like Revitalization, occurs every day as micro events, e.g., marriages, business start ups, and the founding of friendships that bloom into great enterprises.

The two Grand Paths are master models for all change activities. They are presented first to show the grand context in which major issues and conflicts are resolved. In your daily efforts to settle disputes and solve problem, you may use less encompassing paths. The strategies of organizational and community development, re-engineering, search conferences, and many other familiar approaches are partial paths. These paths work with a configuration of modes to select change tools that will solve problems within the boundaries of prudence and efficiency. They are used when you do not need a major change, or when the environment is unprepared for an all encompassing campaign. Ideally, an issue such as the dismissal of a union steward should go beyond a question of rules to determining value and distribution of wealth through labor. Unfortunately, the market does not wait for politics, and such a debate would not get the job done in time for next month's production goals. Ordinary problems can be solved with minor paths, restricted to one or two Boards, that are selected from a variety of paths which match our abilities and the constraints of the situation.

We first describe two Grand Paths, then briefly characterize a sample of minor paths that are currently in use.

THE REVITALIZATION PATH

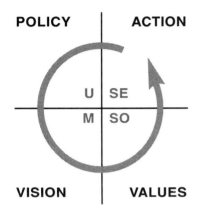

An organization Revitalizes itself by returning to its founding principles to clarify its purpose and goals, and then by building an image that the management can take to the organization's members for implementation. In initiating the act, the organization's executives are admitting that there is a serious threat to the organization—a large loss of markets, a new competitive threat, or lack of adequate management. Revitalization calls for an organization to focus on a program of change that will be carried through from executives to management and down to the work force.

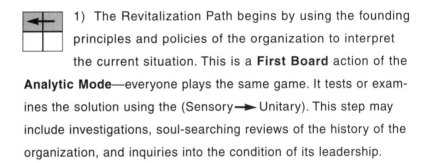

1) The Revitalization Path begins by using the founding principles and policies of the organization to interpret the current situation. This is a **First Board** action of the **Analytic Mode**—everyone plays the same game. It tests or examines the solution using the (Sensory➔Unitary). This step may include investigations, soul-searching reviews of the history of the organization, and inquiries into the condition of its leadership.

2) In the second step, the leader mobilizes energy around a fresh symbol of a belief system. This occurs on the **Second Board** where new rules and policies are created in the **Assertive Mode**. Leaders inspire the managers or team members to accept the new program as it is presented (Unitary➔Mythic). The members are also told what the principles, mission, and core function of the effort are, and how this will effect their jobs. The purpose of this effort is to clarify goals and reestablish the ability of the organization to perform as the executives intend. Often the new vision is an adaptation of a currently prestigious scheme for revitalization such as "re-engineering."

3) In the third step through Revitalization, managers motivate the employees (citizenry) to identify with and value the mission. The path continues through the **Sixth Board** where tools of the **Emergent Mode** are used to facilitate cultural change. Leaders facilitate the employees adopting the revitalized goals and work out ways to accomplish the mission that will satisfy personal and group needs (Mythic➤ Social). Ideally, the effort is "meaning making." The task is to find motivating conditions for attaining policy objectives within restrictions set by the executives. The task can be done by lower level managers or participatively with employees on the Sixth Board.

 4) The final step in a Revitalization Path allocates resources and responsibilities. This occurs on the **Fourth Board** in the marketplace of the **Evaluative Mode**. The final problem solving step is allocating, a Directional Method of action (Social ➤Sensory). The employees revitalize by efficiently taking on the desired work program. They exchange benefits in return for more efficient work. The action is a product of the management's direction and the employees' expertise.

The end results of the Revitalization Path are continuously analyzed on the First Board by an ongoing *testing* (Sensory➤ Unitary) and *designing* (Unitary➤ Sensory) process. The process might begin again if large issues are not solved, or more likely, a minor path may be taken to tie up loose ends.

A Path of Revitalization is most commonly used when responding to major organizational setbacks or adversarial challenges. It calls for organizations to do what they do better. Revitalization retains the organization's "capital" and continuity while reestablishing an effective work force. It achieves the solutions by the familiar "top-down" planning and Directional Methods that are hallmarks of business and administrative management.

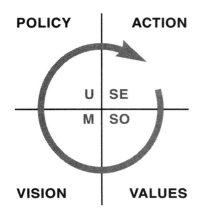

POLICY   **ACTION**

U | SE

M | SO

VISION   **VALUES**

THE RENAISSANCE PATH

The Renaissance Path brings about the rebirth of an organization, creating a new foundation of meaning for the organization or its elements. It abandons established principles, along with the organization's boundaries, purposes, and policies in search of a new identity. The path begins with members sensing a deep discontent with the purposes and performances of an organization, a discontent so deep that they will risk dissolving the present structure to start over again. A Renaissance Path may create a division of a company, refocus a program operating in a community, or initiate a whole new culture.

 1) The Renaissance Path begins by examining what matters to the members. This is the **Evaluative Mode** on the **Fourth Board** where values of the individual members, the organization, and the environment are determined (Sensory ➞ Social). The members review what matters to them as a group. They decide whether they want to work together on a common purpose, or whether they should separate into distinct organizations and programs. The participants may temporarily solve their problem by some reallocation or acceptance, or they may courageously move beyond their dissatisfactions to search for new meaning.

 2) In the second step, organization members work together to create a new identity for the group. In the **Emergent Mode** on the **Sixth Board**, a new culture is evoked by new ideas that reflect new values (Social ➞ Mythic). Members identify a new mission, reframe a technology, and adopt a name and vision for its future. This act of rebirth and creation is an archetypal Mythic act of the Sixth Board.

3) The third step establishes policies that express the new company vision. This is **Assertive Mode** play on the **Second Board** where new rules are established (Mythic→Unitary). Individuals take the offices necessary to formalize legal definitions, gain access to resources, money and property, and contract for work to be done. The new members assert the new rules of conduct, and who is "in" and who is "out." Establishing policies sets the mission, structure, and procedures for the new organization.

 4) The final step within the Renaissance Path puts the new theories and policies into action. This action occurs in the **Analytic Mode** on the **First Board**, where new designs and policies are put into practice (Unitary→Sensory). The operational team translates the new ideas into procedure and actions, using technology and skill to realize a vision in the everyday world.

Renaissance is a dramatic path of change—enlivening, engaging, and sometimes destructive of established foundations. It is used most frequently when establishing new initiatives within existing organizations. The turnabout of Motorola from a packager of consumer communications to an innovative manufacturer exemplifies the courage required to choose deconstruction along the route to a new life. The 3M's Company also popularized this path by inventing the term "Intrapreneurial" activities, calling for continued reinvention from the inside. Increasingly, the path of Renaissance is chosen in response to radically changing environments that question what we once thought was best. Corrections are not enough for the job; we need total organizational transformation, a Renaissance.

In every constructive change effort, no matter how revolutionary your intent, you keep some principles, structures, and authority. To some degree, each path is a Revitalization and a Renaissance of a culture, an organization, or an individual. These pure models are laid out to sharpen your awareness of the ideal processes. You should not let these models delimit your options in practice.

MINOR PATHS OF CHANGE

Over the short history of organizational change strategies (beginning in the 1950's), consultants and organizational designers have introduced a variety of intervention strategies which employ more than a single Mode of Change. These strategies use but a portion of the range of available options. They are responses to the needs of managers who want Paths of Change that are simple and well defined. We provide a condensed description of a five of these methodologies that are widely used with organizational and community change: Socio-Technical Systems Design, Business Process Re-engineering, Interactive Planning, Mediation, and Organization Development. We describe these to illustrate a variety of paths, and to compare and differentiate among them and the grand paths of Revitalization and Renaissance. In showing these minor paths, we wish to support you in choosing paths that are appropriate to your skills, resources, and the needs of the clients.

Problems are solved on a daily basis without needing to correct or transform the whole world. When solving a problem you choose the depth and scope of the issues you want to resolve. If an organization does not have the financial or emotional resources to completely restructure, you focus on solving immediate problems of the day. This usually leads you to a minor path of change for a satisfactory outcome. During most change efforts the big issues of the day are left alone and the immediate problems are addressed.

Every path you take to solve a problem will involve some compromise. While compromises are necessary, frequent changes in direction lead nowhere and waste valuable energy. Setting a firm direction involves risk and requires courage. We can gain experience and skill along the minor paths of change, but true leadership may call for choosing one of the grand paths of Revitalization or Renaissance.

SOCIO-TECHNICAL SYSTEMS DESIGN (STS)

STS evolved out of recognition that solutions designed by outside experts can be weak in comparison to solutions developed by the natural adaptive behaviors of those who do the work.

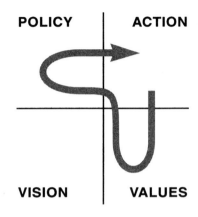

STS is the source of team-based designs such as Open Systems Planning, learning organizations, and various transformative methods that have attracted so much effort in the last decade. It is also a base for industrial democracy. The STS design process calls for a radical release from existing design strategies to optimize the interplay between the worker (Social) and the technical aspects of work (Unitary). STS design aims at a joint optimization of productivity and working conditions for the employees. It is a reaction to low productivity and demeaning working conditions. The early uses of STS were in industries with mass processing such as automobile and paper manufacturers, electronic assembly, and mining.

The STS design path begins by changing policies to reflect the workers' values. It then builds a value consensus among the involved managers and workers to form a contract (Unitary ◄──► Social). The contract sets the limits within which the design work is to be done. Management, workers and the change agents join in an agreement to assure that a deep Renaissance effort will not be undertaken, and that there will be no "surprises" for the executives or labor. In this way, it avoids addressing any emergent ideas that might lead to Renaissance. The design charter minimizes the chance of confrontation with the organization's premises or mission. In a unionized work place, such charters are a major feature of this design ideology, since they protect workers from job loss arising from their own productivity increases. A STS engagement starts with plays on the Third Board setting limits on the extent and direction of redesign.

Following agreement on the scope of design, cross-level teams are formed to jointly design and implement a technically efficient operation (Unitary ◄──► Sensory) that is responsive to the employees' needs and the variances that come from the environment (Social ◄──► Sensory). This is usually based in the operating philosophy that the multi-skilled team, operating with minimal constraints, will be more effective and more life giving than other design philosophies.

A full design effort repeatedly loops through the Social and technical design phases. The loops include technical analyzes which match data and theory (Sensory ◄──► Unitary), and assessing and prioritizing values among the employees (Sensory ◄──► Social). By intent, the Socio-Technical Designer stays away from a Renaissance thrust. There is no expectation of a Mythic recreation or impact on the organizations' structures and policies. Frequently the designers who choose this approach focus on methods that are more technical than socio-emotional, so STS often ends being a form of industrial engineering.

The history of STS is extensively developed in Frans M. van Eijnaten, *The Paradigm that Changed the Work Place*, (1993).

STS design is described simply and practically in James C. Taylor & David F. Felten, *Performance by Design: Sociotechnical Systems in North America*, (1993).

BUSINESS PROCESS RE-ENGINEERING

Re-engineering drives an organization to be more responsive to its external stakeholder: customers, suppliers, neighbors, or competitors. Ideally an organization is Re-engineered by more effectively integrating its internal operations with forces in its environment (Sensory ➤ Unitary). The process begins when executives recognize the failure of the organization to deal with a changing environment. This awareness initiates a scan of the environment and an evaluation of responses for the most cost effective means of serving the various markets. Often this evaluation is done using "benchmarking" followed by a tightly constrained exercise in Renaissance thinking to help the executives explore the alternatives. For example, executives might consider potential solutions at an secret weekend brainstorming session.

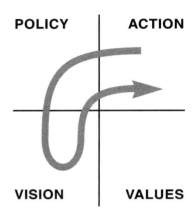

A Re-engineering team, frequently staffed with outside consultants, organizes the executives' findings and asserts a new design principle (Mythic ➤ Unitary). The management team then designs and proposes policy changes (Unitary ➤ Sensory). The path of implementation varies from a simple technical effort calling for new procedures to a full Revitalization path. In all its variations it is a top-down design and implementation process.

The founding book of this scheme is Michael Hammer & James Champy, *Re-engineering the Corporation*, (1993).

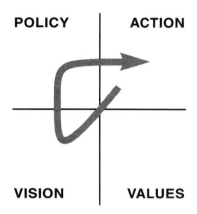

POLICY   **ACTION**

VISION   **VALUES**

INTERACTIVE PLANNING

Interactive planning is the epitome of planning by experts. Experts throughout an organization are combined to discover the most rational plan for effective operation. Play begins on the First Board with multi-level design teams analyzing the present operation and building models of projected future operating conditions (Unitary ◄──► Sensory). Interactive Planning encourages these exhaustive studies to highlight the many "messes" contemporary organizations fall into due to a lack of foresight.

Following the analysis the experts creatively build scenarios of alternative futures. The teams engage in inventive efforts to produce designs that will eliminate messes they foresaw in their analytic studies (Sensory ──► Mythic). Executives select the most promising "futures," then formulate (Mythic ──► Unitary) and implement (Unitary ──► Sensory) the policies into the operations of the organization. It is a Renaissance route without the revaluing that occurs in the Social Reality. This inhibits organizational rebirth, although it often facilitates technological innovation.

Interactive Planning plays primarily on the First and Fifth Boards. That is, the design teams focus on the analysis of symptoms and their creative resolution. The design teams will make an objective note of the organizational values, both economic and personal, and of the politics of the change processes. However, the design process treats these Social concerns as secondary to the analysis and modeling of the organization's work. Thus it is dominantly First Board play with creative ideas implemented assertively.

The founding book of this scheme is Russell L. Ackoff, *Creating the Corporate Future,* (1981).

MEDIATION

Mediation and arbitration address conflicts over rights and interest. Typically mediation is used between parties that have legal contracts with an organization: employees, unions, suppliers, or customers. The process begins with identification of the conflict and its disputants, fact finding (Sensory→Unitary). Then there is an effort to find or set up a procedure for resolution. The created or accepted rules lead to a fair interpretation of the facts (Unitary←→Social). The Unitary pole reduces issues to finding the law or regulation that bears on the facts. The Social pole searches for mutual interests through which they will agree upon a solution to the problem. Mediation usually involves face-to-face work between the two sides, usually with a third neutral party, working toward resolution. The process is formally complete when the parties agree to a modification or an interpretation of the rules that bear on the issue. The solution rebalances the "playing field" with a new distribution of the goods, opportunities, and rights which were in contention. The chosen rules are intended to prevent further conflict over the same kind of issue.

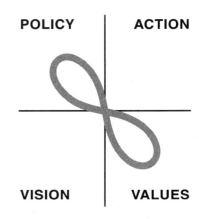

Examples of this path are presented in the work of the Harvard Program on Negotiation. For example: William L. Ury, Jeanne M. Brett, & Stephen B. Goldberg, *Getting Disputes Resolved* (1988).

ORGANIZATIONAL DEVELOPMENT (OD)

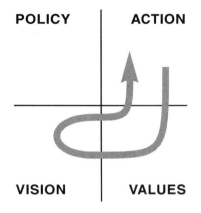

POLICY   ACTION

VISION   VALUES

Organizational Development is more an attitude toward people and organizations than a specific change strategy. However, the strong value based orientation of its practitioners leads to the use of a common set of paths. From the earliest examples change agents interested in OD have given priority to values that enhance the meaning and quality of working life, and secondary attention to those that improve the productivity of the organization. This attention reflects the belief that empowered workers given meaningful jobs are productive, contribute innovations, help to continually lower costs, and are sensitive to the environment of the work. The favored Mode of Change is Evaluative (Sensory ←→ Social).

Like Socio-Technical Systems Design, an OD strategy first calls for building a value consensus among the employees—usually beginning with the values of mid-level managers rather than labor or white collar workers. The initial play is frequently on the Third Board, in order to establish the limits for an acceptable change effort (Unitary ←→ Social).

In subsequent steps, the team designs processes through which they can gain the identified values. These are processes typically to reallocate resources—both employee activities and the range of responsibilities (Social → Sensory). Although it is less frequent, sometimes the redesign of operations takes place with some innovation (Social ←→ Mythic). Successful results on the Fourth Board create new responsibilities and opportunities for employees, focusing on employee working conditions. Participation takes precedence over expertise; that is, play on the Fourth Board dominates that on First Board. This bias may offend the more Analytically oriented managers, industrial engineers, or psychologists. Implementation of the design is likely to follow from the Social allocative demands, rather than the analytic solutions that would appear in a Socio-Technical Design effort.

Most OD change agents do not explicitly deal with the politics of an organization (Social ◄──► Unitary). Initiators tend to avoid issues of power even though it is clear that few value based changes can be implemented without changes in policy, management structure, or even ownership. OD practice avoids issues that confront the unitary powers of the client organizations.

There are many texts in OD consulting. The most popular today is probably Peter Block's work. He has included some discussion of issues of power in *Empowered Manager* (1986). Another view of OD consulting is given by Richard Beckhard and William Pritchard in *Changing the Essence: The Art of Creating and Leading Fundamental Change in Organizations* (1992).

SUMMARY

Every person operates from all of the Realities in the course of a day. So, too, these Paths of Change must touch on each Reality along the trail to resolution. However, as an initiator of change, you will prefer certain Realities and consequently often avoid considering one or more of the Boards. You are likely to habitually use minor or grand paths, such as the ones described here, because you used them successfully in the past. Choice among minor and grand paths should be based on your resources and the situation, rather than your past successes. The *Tools of Change* and methods described in Chapter 6, *Solving the Problem*, are presented as support for your exploration beyond familiar methods of problem solving. These discussions will help you construct Paths of Change and modify these paths while pursuing a solution.

CHAPTER 6

Solving The Problem

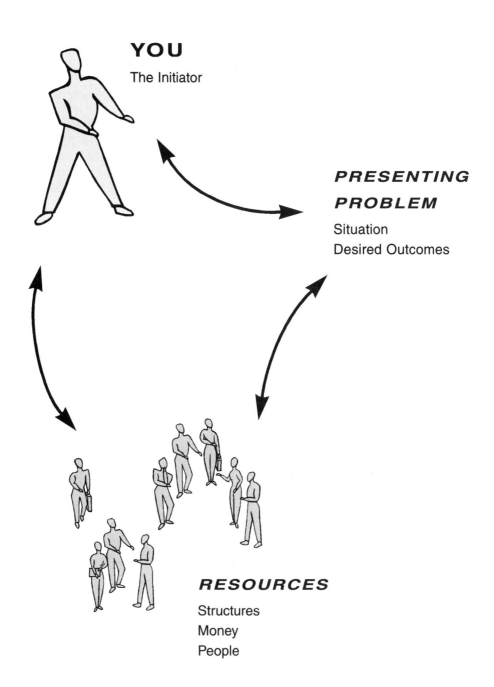

YOU
The Initiator

PRESENTING
PROBLEM
Situation
Desired Outcomes

RESOURCES
Structures
Money
People

FINDING THE METHOD

When selecting a problem-solving method, you must first match the people and resources to the characteristics of the situation, *then* choose the problem-solving method. Problems must be approached with a recognition of their distinctive qualities. Three basic elements must be identified when formulating a problem-solving method—*you*, as the initiator of action, the other *resources* and people involved, and the **presenting problem**.

As the initiator, *you* are the starting point when searching for a solution. Who you are, your particular biases, skills, and knowledge of the situation are all given. These qualities lead you to choose particular Modes of Change that are most familiar to you—ones that you believe will best initiate a problem-solving solution. You choose the initial steps, basing those choices on your Reality preferences and your habitual routines.

The other people who are part of your team are a fundamental portion of your available *resources*. You will use your team members in ways that are dependent on their reality preferences, your reality preferences, the problem formulation, and the stage of the resolution process. However, the skills and biases that they bring to the team are also aspects of the problem. They enable and also restrict the ways in which you approach the problem.

The *presenting problem* begins as a part of the environment. Only when you have explored your preferences and your resources can you decide how to separate out a piece of the environment and call it "the problem." It is likely that you will have to review the problem definition, continually readjusting the boundary between what is central and what is peripheral to your task. The "problem" is a continually emerging question taking new form with each step along the path.

A solution path is a course of continuing questioning—who to involve, what steps to take, when to reevaluate progress, and when has an appropriately stated problem been resolved? Its course is particularly dependent upon the way that you initially formulate your approach. This first choice is critical to the outcome.

"Problems and tasks must be approached with a recognition of their distinctive qualities."

"Your Reality preferences shape how you define the problem and the way you search for resources and solutions."

DIFFERENT APPROACHES

The following example depicts how differently an issue can be approached depending on the "game board" on which the initiator most naturally plays. The example calls for developing a payment system for the workers in a new factory site. It illustrates how differently four managers with varying world views would approach the same situation.

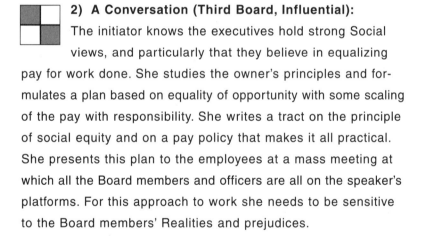

1) A Design Approach (First Board, Analytic):
The initiator identifies the task and selects team members who will help him. He asks them to collect data and do research on currently used wage schemes. Based on their data he designs a plan, then writes a position paper for his supervisor.

2) A Conversation (Third Board, Influential):
The initiator knows the executives hold strong Social views, and particularly that they believe in equalizing pay for work done. She studies the owner's principles and formulates a plan based on equality of opportunity with some scaling of the pay with responsibility. She writes a tract on the principle of social equity and on a pay policy that makes it all practical. She presents this plan to the employees at a mass meeting at which all the Board members and officers are all on the speaker's platforms. For this approach to work she needs to be sensitive to the Board members' Realities and prejudices.

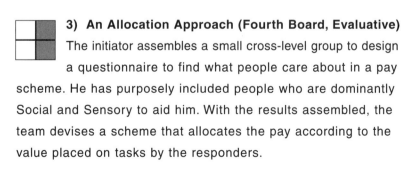

3) An Allocation Approach (Fourth Board, Evaluative)
The initiator assembles a small cross-level group to design a questionnaire to find what people care about in a pay scheme. He has purposely included people who are dominantly Social and Sensory to aid him. With the results assembled, the team devises a scheme that allocates the pay according to the value placed on tasks by the responders.

4) An Evocative Approach (Sixth Board, Emergent)
The initiator forms a small cross-level team and takes them away for a weekend work session. She has explicitly balanced the team on their Realities in order to get the most diverse ideas. Using the *Scenario* and *Visioning* Tools, located on pages 158 and 142, she develops with the team an image of an ideal work situation. Based on this idea the team articulates a new pay scheme that supports the new cultural expectation which arose in the *Visioning* work.

These four examples show how the dominant world views of the initiator and the team members effect the problem-solving process. You cannot fully define the environment, or its participants, until the problem is defined. The process of definition is a continuous spiral, each step being redone as new information and ideas become available. The one aspect of the task that is more or less fixed is the initiator's world view. This is the given in the problem—all other elements can be changed, however difficult it may be. In a long or dramatic situation, even the initiator's world view may be drastically broadened.

DEVELOPING THE TEAM

Creating a team of resource people is as complex a task as selecting the approach to solving a problem. You might find a solution to a problem working alone. However, in today's world, solving any significant issue is as much a task of implementing a solution as it is finding one. At one stage or another, a team of people will be needed. Ideally, you can pick these people based on the world views you want to work with, appropriate skills, and availability. More often you will be in situations where co-workers and team members will be imposed on you by the situation, thereby strongly influencing the path choice.

The less control you have over the selection of co-workers, the more important it is to do extensive developmental work with the given team to create shared awareness of what each member brings to the effort. Certainly this includes shared knowledge of their world views and their competencies, but also their own sense of what the work is about and how their live experience gives meaning to the work. One of the most effective steps in building a change team is having it experience its creation through doing the *Future Perfect* tool on page 184 for the whole task. This experience typically builds trust and a shared sense of value among the members. It produces a sense that the effort will be a shared product of their initiatives.

SELECTING A TOOL

The work is all based on the awareness created by doing the Reality Matrix. With the Matrix complete, the initiator or team can begin to impact the problem situation. The first Mode and direction of engagement has been identified on the Reality Matrix. Now you must select the *Tools of Change*. Go to the *Tools of Change* section and examine each of the tools under your chosen Directional Method. Look for a tool that matches your experience and the circumstances. It is useful if one or more of your resources has experience working with methods similar to the tool. If no one has such experience, it may be best to bring in someone else to direct or aid you in working with that tool. In many cases, you will want to modify the process to fit your situation and sometimes you will find none of the tools provided in the methodology section is suitable. Scanning other tools which use at least one of the same dominant Realities may uncover a tool which you can modify to suit your needs. A number of the tools such as *Mind Mapping* and *Scenario,* on pages 192 and 158, are useful in many situations. With practice you will find it comfortable to create your own variations and instructions as you gain command over the *Tools of Change.*

TAKING ACTION

The action begins the moment you choose to be an initiator, although only when you and your team apply a tool do you begin to make a difference. The action continues along a path, but will seldom be the one you laid out in the first imaging of the situation. At each stage you need to review the appropriateness of the Reality Matrix and of the resources you are bringing to the task. With that awareness again pick appropriate tools on the adjusted path to resolution. Even if you sense that you are unendingly taking detours, it is critical that you stay aware of the path ahead and the direction which you are taking.

The path of instruction in Chapter 6 is concluded with a case, *Elias Cuts Overtime*. Chapter 7 presents two more tales laid out as teaching cases. You may wish to work these to reinforce your own learning and later share them with your team to develop their skills and appreciation for the *Paths of Change*.

Case: Elias Cuts Overtime

SELECTING A PATH

This is a case illustrating the common circumstance of a manager or supervisor confronted with an organizational task that is outside his particular technical focus. He is looking for a means of dealing with a problematic situation and comes to this handbook looking for an appropriate approach and tools for his situation. The case illustrates what methods the supervisor uses when formulating the problem and selecting the appropriate *Tools of Change.*

In this specific situation the supervisor, Elias, is in charge of implementing the policy change. He is responsible for a hospital service group of a dozen skilled workers, ten men and two women. Their work is the maintenance of the air conditioning, lighting, gas flows, and electrical systems. As a group they are highly skilled and self-directing. They require and accept little supervision. Over recent years they have been working considerable overtime. It has provided everyone with 15 to 35% extra income. Elias has just received a management edict to cut overtime for the total group to 5% of the base hours and not more than eight hours for any one person in a week. He has the task of informing the group of the new regulation and implementing it. Elias analyzes his situation by filling out the Reality Matrix. His responses and rationale are noted on the Reality Matrix depicted on the following pages.

ELIAS FILLS OUT THE REALITY MATRIX

1. Please enter your dominant Mode of Change: _____*Analytic*_____

    (Elias is biased toward a Sensory–Unitary Reality with some Social. He is most skilled in the Analytic domain, working from technical competence. As a supervisor he is working on his human relations skills.)

2. Note the team's preferred Modes of Change: _____*Evaluative with some Analytic*_____

    (The team is a mix of Sensory task oriented technicians and younger service-oriented people who are predominantly Social.)

3. Note which of the four Realities are dominant among people who will ultimately authorize or block changes in the Environment of the issue: _____*Unitary management, Social & Sensory employees*_____

    (Hospital management is a benevolent Unitary patriarchy, supportive of human values, but not receptive to initiatives that might disturb the focuses on medicine, fund raising, or cost containment. They are not open to Mythic flights of fancy or Social change. The upper management has many Unitaries and the employees tend toward the Evaluative Mode of working issues.)

4. On what Board do you expect to resolve the issue (circle one):

1ST – Analytic	3RD – Influential	5TH – Inventive
2ND – Assertive	(4TH – Evaluative)	6TH – Emergent

    (The new policy is to be implemented as a marketing "clearing" rule.)

5. On which Boards do you have the opportunity and resources to work the issue (circle all that apply):

(1ST – Analytic)	3RD – Influential	5TH – Inventive
2ND – Assertive	(4TH – Evaluative)	6TH – Emergent

    (Elias does not have a co-leader with Social skill. However, he feels the team's strong Social bias will support his venture into the emotionally expressive realms.)

6. In what direction will you begin your initial path of resolution (circle one):

Revitalization	(Renaissance)	A Lesser Path, along the diagonal direction

    (For example, Elias might choose an Organizational Development path.)

ELIAS' REALITY MATRIX

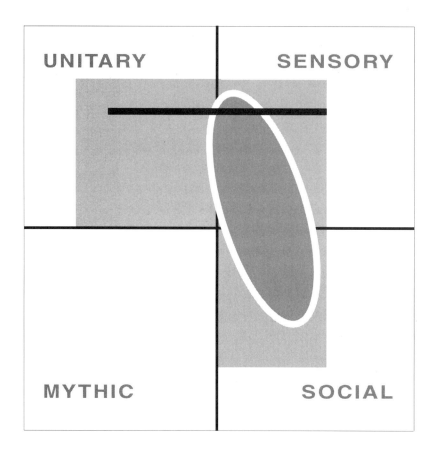

WHEN FILLING OUT THE MATRIX:

*Draw a line that represents **Your dominant Mode** (or Modes) from your Reality Inquiry score:*

*Draw an oval that encompasses the concentration of the **Team's preferred Modes:***

*Shade the quadrants that represent the dominant **Realities** of the people in the **Environment** who will authorize or block changes:*

ELIAS CUTS OVERTIME—SELECTING A TOOL

Elias recognized that there was little chance that the workers would have a matching set of trade-offs between their desire for money versus free time. There was an equally small chance that the team would accept any scheme for allocating overtime that he imposed on them. Any solution Elias designed by himself was certain to meet with disappointment and anger. Elias saw that it was politic to start with the Evaluative Mode of Change (Sensory ◄─► Social) to get the group's participation in settling priorities and work schedules. Although he had not developed skill in working participatively, he sensed that the Social bias of many in the group could be called on to help smooth over the work in the marketplace of the Evaluative Mode.

In the inventory of the Tools of Change section of this workbook there are three tools for determining what is *valued* in a given situation: *Force Field Analysis*, *Story Telling*, and the *Stakeholder Wheel*, located on pages 164, 168, and 166. Elias ruled out *Force Field Analysis*, sensing it could trap the group in arguments about how to place their concerns. *Force Field Analysis* is more useful as a tool to identify group values rather than in finding individual preferences. He saw that *Story Telling* called for skills he had never used and was not sure how they would be received in the larger company community. Elias then noted that the *Stakeholder Wheel* tool requires less interpersonal management skill. It also allows all of the team members to explore their values by projecting their concerns and desires onto other people without the danger of revealing their personal needs. It uses data from the Sensory Reality to locate each person's values in the Social Reality. The Sensory facts elicit the Social value, thereby creating a step in the change process. The output of this exercise is a list of each individual's feelings about overtime work. Reading the *Stakeholder Wheel* tool located on page 166 at this point will help you better understand the decisions Elias and the workers made from this point on.

When the group got together for the first time to deal with the overtime limits, Elias explained the situation and the management's arguments. He proposed that they could still get the work done by a more efficient use of their time if they would look at the work assignment process at the same time they were figuring out how to absorb the cuts demanded by the policy. He explained the *Stakeholder Wheel* tool, indicating that this was the cleanest way he knew to reveal the group member's needs. He was pleased with the way the people went to work immediately on the exercise.

The group shared their "wheels" and recognized that time off and extra money had different values for the members, suggesting that they could build a schedule that would come close to accommodating their preferences for overtime assignments. Elias got "wheels" from the three missing group members and, with the help of two group members, summarized the values each person placed on time versus money. It was clear that each person's trade off varied seasonally. This awareness opened space to accommodate the differing preferences throughout the year.

Having established these evaluations, the team next needed to develop rules for *allocating* (Social→Sensory) the available overtime, with Elias retaining the ultimate responsibility for the assignments. Elias again referred to the *Tools of Change* inventory to choose a tool. He chose the *Resource Allocation* tool associated with the *allocating* Directional Method. See page 172 to locate the *Resource Allocating* tool. With this tool he was able to discuss the selection process with the workers; they had become part of the team in charge of the change process. He shared the preference information and his allocation model with all the workers at the next meeting. They accepted his modified procedure for assigning the overtime work when it is necessary.

Using the *Stakeholder's Wheel* tool and then the *Resource Allocating* tool competed a path, using both Directional Methods within one Mode of Change. The team member's values

(Social) were used to schedule overtime (a Sensory action).
The group members worked with Elias to arrange a schedule so
he would know of their preferences for the coming month. He
took responsibility for making the allocations within the specific
task demands and the overtime limits on the individuals. The
valuing and *allocating* processes became a shared task each
month with Elias retaining ultimate responsibility. Elias noted
that in making this arrangement he was *working with values*,
a new aspect of supervision for him.

**USING WHAT YOU HAVE LEARNED, COMPLETE THE FOLLOWING
REALITY MATRIX AS IT APPLIES TO YOUR SITUATION.**

FILLING OUT THE REALITY MATRIX

Use the following questions to fill out the Reality Matrix on the following page. The questions will aid you when selecting the best Modes and Paths of Change for your problematic situation.

1. Please enter your dominant Mode of Change: _____

    Are you most comfortable using this mode?
    If not, note the mode you prefer using: _____

    Note the mode most typically used by the formal leader of the effort, if this is not your role: _____

2. Note the team's preferred Modes of Change: _____

3. Note which of the four Realities are dominant among people who will ultimately authorize or block changes in the Environment of the issue: _____

4. On what Board do you expect to resolve the issue (circle one):

1ST – Analytic	3RD – Influential	5TH – Inventive
2ND – Assertive	4TH – Evaluative	6TH – Emergent

5. On which Boards do you have the opportunity and resources to work the issue (circle all that apply):

1ST – Analytic	3RD – Influential	5TH – Inventive
2ND – Assertive	4TH – Evaluative	6TH – Emergent

6. In what direction will you begin your initial path of resolution (circle one):

Revitalization	Renaissance	A Lesser Path, along the diagonal direction

THE REALITY MATRIX

UNITARY	SENSORY
MYTHIC	SOCIAL

WHEN FILLING OUT THE MATRIX:

*Draw a line that represents **Your dominant Mode** (or Modes) from your Reality Inquiry score:*

*Draw an oval that encompasses the concentration of the **Team's preferred Modes:***

*Shade the quadrants that represent the dominant **Realities** of the people in the **Environment** who will authorize or block changes:*

CHAPTER 7

Two Cases

TWO CASES: DESIGNING A PATH OF CHANGE

The following two cases are designed to give you practice in finding and selecting appropriate *Paths* and *Tools of Change*. The cases are designed for you to use either as an individual or in a group. They can be used progressively while learning the material or as practice to reinforce what you learned after working through the book.

CASE #1 - ABSENTEEISM'S HIDDEN AGENDA

SWANSIE COMPANY HISTORY:

The Swansie Company is a national food packager. It has many established canning works around the country. This particular site in the company is one of the oldest, having been founded before World War II. Much of the work takes place on production lines where each operation depends on the speed of the departments 'up the line.' If one section is slow to start up in the morning, everything beyond it is short of work causing delays and inefficiency. The work is highly routine: preparing foods, mixing sauces, canning, labeling, and shipping. Although the plant has been continually modernized it is not state-of-the-art. The character of the work has not changed greatly since 1960, and many of the employees have worked at the plant most of that time. The general economy of the industry is good, but presently is in a moderate recession such as experienced in the early 1990's. Quite a few people in town have worked the canning lines over the years. Many have gone on to raise families and run their own shops, but are still available for canning work when the demand arises.

The labor contract has two years to run and relations with the union are always tenuous. The union's executive committee is composed of many older workers and some younger militant workers. The plant is in a region that has had a history of strife between unionized workers and management.

"If they aren't reliable we'll have to get rid of them." This was the position of Phil Schwartz, the frustrated plant manager. "Our production depends on having the work force at their stations at 7:15, five days a week. When one person doesn't show up the whole line is slowed down. We can't afford to have a back-up employee for every job on the line."

The new manager of the packing department, Joe Williams, had just fired three women for excessive absences. He was within his rights under the Union contract, but the community and the Union steward were in an uproar over the event. Things came to a boil when personnel filled the positions with three women who lived in the neighborhood of the fired employees. The neighbors called them "scabs" for taking the jobs. The police had to settle a fight between two of the husbands. The union leaders had to protest. Discussion with community representatives could contribute greatly to understanding their issues and might suggest new avenues for resolution. However, the labor counsel indicated such involvement might raise legal issues far beyond the questions of absentee firing.

YOUR INVOLVEMENT:

You are the Human Resource Manager for the site. You have been in this position for a couple of years and have earned the respect of the site managers. You heard of the problem from Joe Williams, the packing manager, your wife who heard from co-workers at the community center, and now from the Union steward who has asked for a meeting. What steps do you take to lead to a *Path of Change*?

What would you do? What further information do you need? Make some notes about your ideas.

DATA YOU NEED TO COMPLETE THE REALITY MATRIX:

YOUR DOMINANT MODE: Determined by your score on the Reality Inquiry.

YOUR TEAM'S PREFERRED MODE:

Your immediate resources include the Labor counsel, your staff, and the Plant manager. Later you may come to view some of these people as part of the problem rather than as resources.

1. The labor relations attorney is a strong Unitary, thoroughly knowledgeable of the contract terms and the means of enforcement. He recently came to the site from a corporate headquarters position.

2. Your staff consists of two younger people. Joan is 37 and married. She has been with the company for one year. Her Reality Inquiry score shows a strong Emergent bias (Social ◄──► Mythic) Jimmie started as a laborer, was then a union steward, and was subsequently sent by the company to get a degree in counseling. He joined you three years ago. His preference is Evaluative (Sensory ◄──► Social), and he is a good "schmoozer" and negotiator.

3. The Plant Manager, Phil Schwartz, is a company man with 20 years in management and an MBA from Indiana University. He has come up through production with a four year stint with the Industrial Engineering Department. His preference is Analytic (Unitary ◄──► Sensory) with a back-up in the Mythic Reality. He is a high energy task oriented manager.

REALITIES IN THE ENVIRONMENT:

1. Joe Williams is in his mid-thirties and is on his first assignment as a department manager. He is the new manager of the packing department. He has good experience in line management and has a degree in business administration. He is a strong Sensory with a Social back-up. He and his wife grew up in a nearby town and have now returned after being at a Southern plant for a few years.

2. The Management Committee consists of department managers, Phil and the plant manager's staff. They are all older than Joe and several have been passed over for promotion. Their dominant Reality is Unitary with Sensory and Social back-ups.

3. The Union Executive Committee is made up of Swansie employees, although the president of the Union left the company to be a full time union officer. He is 60 and came up through the ranks of the union. He is tough-minded and concerned with social justice. His dominant style is Influential (Social ◄──► Unitary). His colleagues are three women, apparently also Influential (Social ◄──► Unitary) and four men who have scattered world views.

4. The corporate management at the higher levels is a copy of the plant management. Senior level management is more Sensory and aggressive. The CEO uses an Inventive (Sensory ◄──► Mythic) style of leadership and is interested in change; he is not particularly charismatic.

WHAT APPROACH WILL YOU TAKE?

Consider all the information that affects your situation. Reflect upon the outcomes you would expect by following each of the three paths.

1. **RENAISSANCE:** Look at the basic values in the situation to come up with a new work relation.

2. **REVITALIZATION:** Reestablish the proper relation of authority in the work place and then find ways to moderate the impact on the community.

3. **A LESSER PATH:** Reframe the problem.

You now have enough information to complete the Reality Matrix. Fill in the form now.

FILLING OUT THE REALITY MATRIX

Use the following questions to fill out the Reality Matrix on the following page. The questions will aid you when selecting the best Modes and Paths of Change for your problematic situation.

1. Please enter your dominant Mode of Change: _____

    Are you most comfortable using this mode?
    If not, note the mode you prefer using: _____

    Note the mode most typically used by the for-
    mal leader of the effort, if this is not your role: _____

2. Note the team's preferred Modes of Change: _____

3. Note which of the four Realities are dominant
    among people who will ultimately authorize or
    block changes in the Environment of the issue: _____

4. On what Board do you expect to resolve the issue (circle one):

    | 1ST – Analytic | 3RD – Influential | 5TH – Inventive |
    | 2ND – Assertive | 4TH – Evaluative | 6TH – Emergent |

5. On which Boards do you have the opportunity and resources to work the issue (circle all that apply):

    | 1ST – Analytic | 3RD – Influential | 5TH – Inventive |
    | 2ND – Assertive | 4TH – Evaluative | 6TH – Emergent |

6. In what direction will you begin your initial path of resolution (circle one):

    | Revitalization | Renaissance | A Lesser Path, along the diagonal direction |

THE REALITY MATRIX

UNITARY	SENSORY
MYTHIC	SOCIAL

WHEN FILLING OUT THE MATRIX:

*Draw a line that represents **Your dominant Mode** (or Modes) from your Reality Inquiry score:*

*Draw an oval that encompasses the concentration of the **Team's preferred Modes**:*

*Shade the quadrants that represent the dominant **Realities** of the people in the **Environment** who will authorize or block changes:*

ACTUAL PROCESS AND OUTCOME:

In the source case for Absenteeism's Hidden Agenda the dominant Reality of the Human Resource manager, your assigned role, was Social, thus indicating that the most favorable approach was along the Influential route. The desired outcome was to create a new value that responds to the needs of both the community and workplace.

One possibility was for you to do the *Pseudo-Quotes* tool on page 152 chosen from the *persuading* Directional Method. However, the Labor Counsel blocked the Human Resource manager (your role) from involving community people. To get an estimation of the community values, a session was set up with the union executive committee and the plant management team. They did the *Story Telling* tool see page 168 to determine the community stakeholder's values. They simulated a conversation between a line supervisor and an employee, where the employee called in at 7:10 AM saying she was unable to come to work.

As the dialog of this story unfolded the supervisor was obviously most distressed because 7:10 AM was too late to get a replacement in time to start the line. Very quickly someone in the group suggested that the problem was not the absence of the worker but that the supervisor was unprepared to replace her. The problem was getting a replacement in time. That idea lead to reframing the issue and the need for the workers to act responsibly if they wanted management to make room for their home life. They recognized that it was a joint community-management issue. By clearly articulating the values, the issue evolved into a task of modifying the current administrative rules to allow workers to be absent when they gave the supervisor sufficient notice. This reframed the problem statement to be "finding a policy that would allow a worker to take needed time off without reducing the long-run effectiveness of the production process."

The group turned the task of designing an *Action Plan,* on page 124, over to a committee. This work was an Analytic effort that occurred after persuading the management-union group that the new values would be useful to them.

This is an example of a minor path that began in a Renaissance direction. The stakeholder's insights reframed the problem into a Social ➤ Unitary issue where the new values were articulated. The management and union executives then cooperated in designing and testing (Unitary ◀▶ Sensory) the new policy within the current labor contract—a First Board solution.

End of Absenteeism's Hidden Agenda

CASE #2 - "SO, WHERE'S THE SCHEDULE?"

DISCORP COMPANY HISTORY:

Three years ago Discorp was a company clearly heading for bankruptcy. Its hi-tech products were months late in coming to the market and overpriced for the features they offered. Once on the market they were not delivered on time. The morale in the company was deteriorating and the company was losing top talent, both among the managers and the technologists. The CEO, seeing the inevitable, resigned.

The Discorp Board initiated an intense and well-directed search to find a seasoned CEO who could revive a company that had a quality product in a growing market but was failing due to antiquated management processes. They choose Alonzo, age 47. He began his career as a sales engineer, retrained at MIT in the Sloan Management Program, and has since had five years experience as a CEO of a smaller company. On taking the job Alonzo immediately held an open forum meeting that all employees attended in person or via video network. He talked of his philosophy of aggressive openness and his wish to bring all the employees into "sync" with his dreams of a quality operation.

In the following weeks Alonzo was highly visible around the offices and plant sites, questioning, listening, testing ideas. He was bringing new energy and direction to the employees. Three months into his presidency he released two vice-presidents and four other senior executives. He replaced only one of the VP's and one manager, setting the stage for a gradual reduction of the management hierarchy. Alonzo then began a broad reeducation program, continually working together with management and other employees to introduce new ideas for an open system organization and team based management, introducing the vocabulary of "the new paradigm." He began a series of multi-level task forces to find new ideas that would turn the company around. They reported to company-wide conferences for their adoption. Alonzo reinforced his desires that the company have a system with almost completely open access to information by insuring all jobs would be posted, team work would be introduced as appropriate, and supervision would be phased out as rapidly as the employees wished to take on the responsibility. Most of all, the employees would be encouraged to aggressively search for new ways to improve the products, the delivery, and the quality of work. That was nine months ago.

YOUR INVOLVEMENT

Alonzo, the CEO, has called on you, an outside consultant known for your work with open systems and high performing companies, for advice and support. After the usual familiarities, he opens by describing his vision of the company's operation including the ideas listed above. Then, abruptly he says, "But it's not working! Communications aren't open, schedules haven't improved, morale may even be down. There is no flow. I have heard excuses and explanations from every level in the company. I could recall them for you, but I would prefer to have you wander around using whatever magic you have to find out for yourself. Then come back and we'll make it work together as a company."

So, with permission to poke anywhere, a few politically correct introductions, and a guide assigned from the Administrative VP's office, you head out into Discorp.

What would you do? What further information do you need? Make some notes about your ideas.

DATA YOU NEED TO COMPLETE THE REALITY MATRIX:

YOUR REALITY PREFERENCES: Determined by your score on the Reality Inquiry.

YOUR RESOURCES:

1. You have a small consulting company, skilled in aspects of organizational design and development, production management, market strategizing, stakeholder relations, etc.

2. Your Discorp guide is clearly a Sensory with Social back-up. She is full of facts and is energetic in making connections to people and aspects of the business.

3. Alonzo, the CEO, is clearly Inventive (Mythic◄──►Sensory) with a good Social back-up, but also with an avoidance of the Unitary world view.

REALITIES IN THE ENVIRONMENT:

1. The Plant and Engineering: A brief visit indicates that the work force is partly a younger group that enjoys participation and use the Evaluative style (Sensory◄──►Social), and partly older employees that likes the idea of teams but is not keen on change. The older employees appear to have a Unitary bias.

2. Management: The management, many of whom were promoted from the supervisory ranks or from technical positions, are very Analytically oriented, perhaps more Unitary than Sensory. They are a multiracial group and almost all men.

The workers were disappointed at they way things were going after Alonzo took over. A typical story came from David, a team coordinator in the preparation and packing department: "It's Tuesday! So where is the schedule for shipments? We can't plan the work-week without it. McAlister (sales department manager) hasn't released it yet. Janet said he took it for review Friday at noon and she hasn't gotten it back and can't send me a copy until he approves it. I asked Jim, my boss, to get it; he agreed, but that was yesterday noon. He's not around this morning, and I still don't have the schedule!"

Some other comments came from the Power Supply section: "They want us to deliver state-of-the-art boxes that are integrated, that are in 'sync' with the new amplifiers. But the Section head has asked us not to disturb the team working on the product; he would answer all our questions himself. He's not a 'techie,' so we keep getting only part of the story and, well, we don't trust that he understands half of what we are talking about." And, "I was promised I could go to the ASEE Power conference. A couple of weeks before I checked with the education section they hadn't even received authorization for me to go. Finally, I got the permission and got there, but by then the reservations were messed up,..."

On asking what these people have done about the discomfort, you hear that they have held meetings with the managers of the various involved departments. They always get explanations for why things haven't worked in the past and promises that things will work better in the future.

WHAT APPROACH WILL YOU TAKE?

Consider all the information that affects your situation. Reflect upon the outcomes you would expect by following each of the three paths.

1. **RENAISSANCE:** Democratically develop relations between the workers and managers.

2. **REVITALIZATION:** Have managers accept the new organizational process.

3. **A LESSER PATH:** Reframe the problem.

You now have enough information to complete the Reality Matrix. Fill in the form now.

FILLING OUT THE REALITY MATRIX

Use the following questions to fill out the Reality Matrix on the following page. The questions will aid you when selecting the best Modes and Paths of Change for your problematic situation.

1. Please enter your dominant Mode of Change: _____

    Are you most comfortable using this mode?
    If not, note the mode you prefer using: _____

    Note the mode most typically used by the for-
    mal leader of the effort, if this is not your role: _____

2. Note the team's preferred Modes of Change: _____

3. Note which of the four Realities are dominant
    among people who will ultimately authorize or
    block changes in the Environment of the issue: _____

4. On what Board do you expect to resolve the issue (circle one):

    1ST – Analytic   3RD – Influential   5TH – Inventive

    2ND – Assertive   4TH – Evaluative   6TH – Emergent

5. On which Boards do you have the opportunity and resources to work the issue (circle all that apply):

    1ST – Analytic   3RD – Influential   5TH – Inventive

    2ND – Assertive   4TH – Evaluative   6TH – Emergent

6. In what direction will you begin your initial path of resolution (circle one):

    Revitalization   Renaissance   A Lesser Path, along
                                                 the diagonal direction

THE REALITY MATRIX

UNITARY	SENSORY
MYTHIC	SOCIAL

WHEN FILLING OUT THE MATRIX:

*Draw a line that represents **Your dominant Mode** (or Modes) from your Reality Inquiry score:*

*Draw an oval that encompasses the concentration of the **Team's preferred Modes:***

*Shade the quadrants that represent the dominant **Realities** of the people in the **Environment** who will authorize or block changes:*

ANALYSIS OF THE CHANGE EFFORT

The change process was initiated before you got to Discorp. That is, the corporate Board, in firing the CEO when there were signs of failure, initiated a small Renaissance loop. The Board beheaded their organization and brought in a new leader, Alonzo. Unfortunately, he could not establish his leadership and complete the loop of the organization's rebirth. The managers sensed him as a potential enemy from the beginning. It is easy to surmise that under such circumstances the managers were entrenched in the political games of the Third Board, ready to play games to insure that Alonzo could not gain advantage by further firings or eroding of their power.

It became clear that there was a deep blockage between the managers and the Alonzo ideas, that the managers were sandbagging the workers and Alonzo. The managers' power positions allowed them to deny any open discussion of problems, while continuing to undercut the open communication policies that Alonzo preached. The employees could not mount an open attack on the manager's attitude and Alonzo seemed powerless to effect a change. That is why the CEO called you in.

STEPS YOU TOOK

As the consultant, you recognized that a deep conflict had arisen between Alonzo's ideas and the managers' needs. You saw that the managers had entrenched political positions on the Third Board. You decided that the only way to resolve their conflict was to remove them from the political games of the Third Board and play more openly on the Sixth Board where value issues can be shared. You suggested that a small representative group of the disillusioned operating people get together to see what they could do.

The group did a Reality Matrix exercise that suggested they all shared the Sensory Reality. However, they noted that neither the worker's task oriented approach (which might use the *Action Plan* tool on page 124) nor Alonzo's Mythic leadership had been sufficient to establish new ways of thinking, a new organizational form, or a new set of values. A new plan was not enough; they needed a *new culture*. The group saw that they would need to return to an earlier stage of their path to explore and share values among all the organization's membership.

CHOOSING A TOOL

The group anticipated that simply inviting the managers to work with labor at this point was likely to result in the same sandbagging. As the consultant you needed to reveal a broader understanding of the managers' needs and concerns. As the managers recognized the blockage, they shifted toward the Sixth Board where new cultures are created. They choose to approach the problem with a *converting* tool (Unitary➤ Social) of the Influential Mode, oddly in this case, to convert themselves.

The first *converting* tool within the Influential Mode of the Tools of Change is *Getting the Message* located on page 156. It assumes that a total quality philosophy has been endorsed by the organization.

The second tool within that same section is *Scenario* from page 158. It has the managers work toward gaining agreement on the new organizational structure and policies by creating acceptable scenarios. This approach seemed appropriate so the group organized a Scenario session a few days later.

WHAT WOULD YOU DO?

Read the *Scenario* tool on page 158. Do a simulation of this exercise to get a sense of what happens when you begin to think along the lines of creating acceptable possibilities through a *Scenario*. When you have completed the exercise consider continuing in this direction on a Renaissance path. A Renaissance path would continue through the Mythic Reality where new visions are created and then onto the Unitary Reality where issues of policy setting are debated. What would you do?

If you chose a Renaissance path, you might continue with an *evoking* tool (Social➤ Mythic) from the Emergent Mode that would help the managers adopt and share the CEO's dream with labor. Then, you might *establish* (Mythic➤ Unitary) the new company image through policies that the managers would carry out. Read the tools that *evoke* and *establish* from the *Tools of Change*. What would you do? Which tools would you choose?

A POSSIBLE PATH

The managers would probably still he hesitant about joining labor in a new effort after completing the *Scenario*. The managers might participate in creating an image symbolizing the entire employee population's values in order to join the rest of the group. Since the managers are primarily Analytically oriented this step would be difficult. The consultant (your role) might select the most structured of the *evoking* tools (Social➤Mythic) the *Core of Intent,* located on page 190, to assist the managers in this unfamiliar method of problem solving. Of the various *establishing* tools (Mythic➤Unitary), *Visioning*, located on page 142, seems most appropriate for the second step of this path. It avoids confrontation and argument, yet can produce an empathic flow of ideas and actions.

WHAT ALONZO DID

Alonzo , the CEO, intended to begin a Revitalization path. He imposed his first action into the Social domain. The managers needed to accept the new values before they could share Alonzo's ideas. Alonzo brought the work force into accord by *converting* them to his new policy (Unitary➤Social). Having gained their acceptance he then *established* a new policy (Mythic➤Unitary). The policies could then be directly implemented and *designed* (Unitary➤Sensory). Notice the path seems to have skipped a step, jumping from the Social to the Mythic. Alonzo took a rather autocratic stance by not having the employees help him formulate the new policy. There was no participative involvement from the workers. This denial of the contributions of others is typical of a strong Mythic and can create problems.

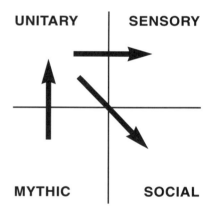

A change process calls for ingenuity and sensitivity to the situations. In practice the paths of Revitalization and Renaissance are seldom simple, and frequently one path requires some of the qualities we associate with the other.

How would you construct a path to insure that the changes are affected? What tools would you use? Think through the rationale for your choices and anticipate the outcomes.

End of "So, where's the schedule?"

TOOLS OF CHANGE

INVENTORY

OF TOOLS

MODES OF CHANGE	DIRECTIONAL METHODS	TOOL	PAGE
EVALUATIVE	**VALUE** Sensory → Social	*Dialogue* *Force Field Analysis* *Stakeholder Wheel* *Story Telling*	*162* *164* *166* *168*
	ALLOCATE Social → Sensory	*Move to Where it Matters* *Resource Allocation*	*170* *172*
INVENTIVE	**INDUCE** Sensory → Mythic	*Brainstorming* *Metaphor* *New Game* *Role Assignments*	*176* *178* *180* *182*
	REALIZE Mythic → Sensory	*Future Perfect* *Lotus Blossom*	*184* *186*
EMERGENT	**EVOKE** Social → Mythic	*Core of Intent* *Mind Mapping* *Search Conference*	*190* *192* *194*
	FACILITATE Mythic → Social	*Co-generation* *Innovation Process*	*196* *198*

LISTING OF TOOLS A–Z

THE ANALYTIC MODE

The Analytic Mode is based on the observation of principles and facts. It depends on reasoning. Theory and the information available to the senses are used to identify solutions, predict implications, and evaluate outcomes. Play is on the First Board, where performance is optimized through operational means within established rules, policies, and strategies. Change tends to occur within existing organizational structures and systems of belief, such as the existing framework of science. Change occurs within the Analytic Mode by using two Directional Methods, to Design and Test. Individuals with a task-oriented leadership style will tend to cycle between Designing and Testing as their preferred approach to planning, resolving conflicts, and affecting change.

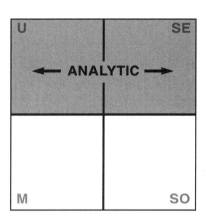

DIRECTIONAL METHODS

DESIGN

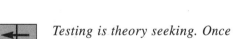

The Designing Directional Method puts a theory, principle, or strategy into practice. If the theory is sufficiently inclusive of the situation and if accurate measurements exist, the theory leads to the appropriate action steps.

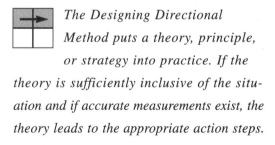

TEST

Testing is theory seeking. Once principles, truths, or theories are found that fit the situation, insights are gained by making connections with similar phenomena. Interpretations and predictions can be made from this information.

DESIGN

PURPOSE: *To design a plan that puts into practice a strategy, theory, or principle, reflecting the reality of available resources.*

OUTCOMES: *A specific set of steps and objectives with resources assigned, carrying the strategy into practice.*

SAMPLE USES:

• *One-time events, such as celebrations, sporting events, or facility moves.*

• *Special maintenance tasks, surveys, and inventory recounts.*

ACTION PLAN

Planning is such a central part of organizational life that it comes into your work every day. This exercise is designed for local planning or for planning in new or small organizations.

1. **Write a statement identifying the strategy or principles to be put into action.** For example, "Have the book ready for publication on January 1, 1997."

2. **Have your group brainstorm a list of tasks** (including duties and objectives), **and a list of resources required** to accomplish these tasks. (See the *Brainstorming* tool located on page 176.)

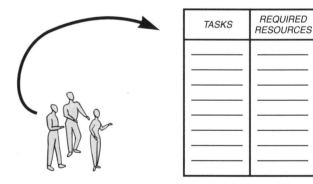

TASKS	REQUIRED RESOURCES

3. **Check the list of tasks against the strategy, and the required resources against those available.** Revise as needed. If there is a significant mismatch, redesign the plan against the strategy or against the resource requirements. Revise until a match is achieved. If it still fails, bring in new people for a fresh brainstorming session.

STRATEGY ←→ TASKS   RESOURCES ←→ RESOURCES
REQUIRED   AVAILABLE

4. Chart the work flow by establishing a time line that corresponds to each task within the plan. Verify that each task is feasible by the required date. If not, return to Brainstorming. The following example charts the progression of selecting a new computer system for an office.

IDENTIFY NEED FOR A
NEW COMPUTER SYSTEM

REVIEW CURRENT SYSTEM

DETERMINE SPECIFIC NEEDS
RESEARCH NEW SYSTEMS
DETERMINE AVAILABLE FUNDS

PURCHASE NEW EQUIPMENT
REORGANIZE OFFICE

INSTALL NEW SYSTEMS
TRAIN EMPLOYEES

JAN.   FEB.   MAR.   APR.   JUNE...

5. List the tasks to be assigned, who is responsible for each task, what resources are available, when the resources will be needed, and when the tasks will be completed. Remember to include people, money, and materials. Organize the information onto a chart:

TASK	PERSON RESPONSIBLE	REQUIRED RESOURCES	RESOURCES NEEDED BY	DATE TASK COMPLETED

6. Follow up on the Action Plan you designed. Plans fail if assignments and up-to-date status reports are not publically shared information. Such reports are best maintained with computer-aided planning programs.

 DESIGN

GROUP SIZE: *The total involvement may be over 100, but task groups should be small groups of 7-9 people. Beyond this size a facilitator is required to manage the process.*

TIME REQUIREMENTS: *Varies with the scope of the task, but rushing the effort usually produces unworkable plans.*

SPACE FACILITIES: *Work area can range from a wall chart, to a set of conference rooms with computer support.*

PREPARATION: *The leader and change agent should have specific training and experience in planning.*

EQUIPMENT: *Planning should be supported by computerized programs.*

DESIGN

PURPOSE: *To separate different types of causal sources, insuring the best formulation of the problem and a practical solution.*

OUTCOMES: *A systematic scan of possible causes and assignment of priorities for engaging with those causes.*

COMMENTS: *This tool is best used with people who are familiar with the six Boards of Play from Chapter 4.*

SAMPLE USES:
• *Starting a design or change process in a well understood environment.*

CAUSING EFFECTS

What caused "X"? Your answer depends on your world view, the views held by other people, and the situation. Your ability to work effectively depends on the match of your resources with how you see "X".

1. **Agree on a brief statement of the issue or desired outcome.** Use a brainstorming technique to form the statement if needed.

2. **Divide the participants into groups of 2-3 people.** Give each group a stack of blank cards. Have the participants write one short phrase on each card describing what they think caused "X". Each causal statement can refer to the whole problem or just one aspect of the problem. After each person has completed their statements, share the participants statements within the sub-groups.

3. **Determine on which Board of Play each of your causal statements belongs.** For example: a "parts shortage" is on the 1st board. "Forgetting to order parts in time," is on the 3th board. "Wanting a newer part," is on the 4th board.

Six Boards of Play

1st: Materials, machines, products & service design.
2nd: Rules, procedures, instructions, constraints & authorities.
3rd: Responsibilities, fairness & morality.
4th: Relations, desires, rewards & allocations.
5th: (Omitted because *invention* is part of the solution.)
6th: Meanings, understanding & spirit.

4. **Have sub-groups enter the causal statements on the section of the "feather diagram,"** shown below, representing the Board of Play where the statements belong.

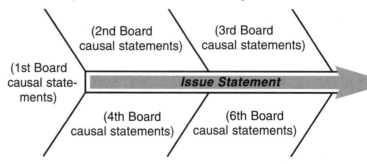

5. Collect the sub-group work to form an overall feather diagram. Build a wall-sized feather diagram like the example below that the whole group can see. Check to make sure the causal statements are on the proper boards and that they are not duplicated.

6. Reflect on the feather diagram. On what boards do most of the statements appear? Do aspects of the same problem occur on two or more boards? For example, on the previous page, the parts shortage had both technical and personal causes. Fill out a Reality Matrix for your issue. Compare the strengths and weaknesses of the Reality Matrix to the feather diagram. A good match signals a good implementation. A poor match suggests the solution will be ineffective.

7. See if any causal statements can be restated on another board where you might be better able to work with it. For example, if your group works better with 3rd Board issues, a 4th Board statement such as "One-way communication," could be restated as "Top-down power," a 3rd Board statement. This produces a step-by-step reframing toward a solution.

8. Reorganize the statements on the wall-sized feather diagram if necessary. Use the diagram as a guide to organizing the problem-solving effort, setting boundaries on what to do, putting tasks in order of priority and sequence, and assigning tasks to individuals and groups. This approach to design works with stable and well understood issues. In a more complex setting use it to organize what is known, leaving messy issues for more exploration.

DESIGN

GROUP SIZE: *One person to many.*

TIME REQUIREMENTS: *One hour to a half day.*

SPACE FACILITIES: *Conference room with wall space.*

PREPARATION: *The more the participants know of the problem environment the better.*

EQUIPMENT: *Feather diagrams: desk size and wall chart size.*

DATA: *None beyond the knowledge held by participants.*

9. Example: A feather diagram from a manufacturing operation.

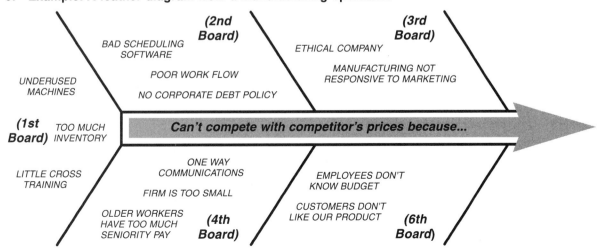

DESIGN

PURPOSE: *To explore what "qualities" matter to people when making choices on issues.*

OUTCOMES: *A list of attributes that are attractive or unattractive when finding a solution to a problem.*

SAMPLE USES:

• *Getting started on a task in an unfamiliar situation.*

• *Helping people who are not used to problem solving define what it is they want to achieve.*

EXTRACTING THE QUALITIES

Many disputes arise because people are not clear about "qualities." If someone says, "It is hot," are they speaking of temperature, popularity, or illegality? Qualities are the dimensions of evaluation, for example, cost, flexibility, color, and tone. Clarifying the dimensions of an activity makes it easier to understand the origins of a conflict and the direction for resolution. This tool works to clarify a situation; it does not provide a solution or a consensus.

1. What are the possible solutions?

Have the entire group develop a statement defining the problem. Divide into groups of 3-6 people. *Brainstorm* to develop a number of initial possible solutions (see page 176 for the *Brainstorming* tool). Have everyone create at least one possible solution without prejudging whether it is particularly good or feasible. Typically this exercise produces 15-30 possible solutions from the entire group. Briefly present each idea either orally or by writing them on a flip chart so that everyone is able to "sense" the outcome of the proposals.

2. What are the best and worst ideas?

From the possible solutions have the entire group select (by voting, ranking, or acclaim) a diverse set of 3 proposals which seem to be particularly attractive and 3 that are particularly unattractive.

3. Role playing scenarios, the best ideas.

Select one of the attractive proposals. Identify two people within the scenario whose roles would be relevant to the idea's acceptance. For example, a CEO and a division manager, where the manager wants the CEO to approve an idea. Begin the role playing with the manager saying why the idea is attractive. The CEO's role is to draw out the advantages, critically or supportively. Have an observer write the pros and cons on a flip chart. After about 5 minutes of role playing, examine and discuss the list of arguments, clarifying and expanding the ideas. Repeat this activity with a second proposal and with different players. Repeating the activity a third time will probably be enough to identify the most significant attractive qualities.

4. Role playing scenarios, the worst ideas.

Repeat the role playing exercise, having the group follow the same steps, but advocating the 3 worst ideas.

Role playing example: Ann is the CEO and Bill is the manager. Bill wants Ann to approve an idea.

Bill: *"I like the idea because it is elegant."*
Ann: *"What do you mean by elegant?"*
Bill: *"Well, it looks simple and has a nice form."*
Ann: *"Why should it look simple?"*
Bill: *"It will be easier to develop and produce, and the customer will clearly see its function."*
Ann: *"Fair enough. Now what about nice form?"*
Bill: *"It should appeal to the customers."*
Ann: *"Do you know what they like?"*

Bill has argued the qualities of *complexity* and *functionality*. He is now looking for the quality that underlies "nice form."

 DESIGN

GROUP SIZE: *5 or more people. Divide larger groups into smaller groups of 3-6 people when brainstorming.*

TIME REQUIREMENTS: *A couple hours.*

SPACE FACILITIES: *A conference room*

EQUIPMENT: *Flip charts.*

SOURCE: *Tassoul. (1992).*

5. *Extracting the Qualities.*

Review the notes written on the flip charts. Extract the qualities to which people referred in their scenarios. In the example above when Bill said "simple" you have to be clear whether he means *functional* or *low complexity*? When someone said an idea is "cool" does that refer to *marketability* or the *style*? Designs cannot be completed or issues resolved if your members do not agree on what dimensions are important.

Resolve the questions of dimension. Then list the qualities on a new sheet. *Notice it makes no difference whether the quality appeared in a worst or best case scenario.* Qualities in both make us aware of what we care about.

6. Designing a program or product:

The next step in a design process is to rank the importance of the qualities, that is, the dimensions of a solution. Note that the ranking is of the dimensions, not the level. So it is "temperature" and "functionality" with which you are concerned, not "hot" and "simple." Later as you put together a solution you will become clearer on what levels of the particular dimensions are required or desirable as well as how much weight should be given to the dimension. For example, "complexity" is a far less important dimension than "customer appeal." Now you might go on to a tool in the Emergent or Inventive modes.

TEST

AFFINITY DIAGRAMS

PURPOSE: *To find a pattern or classification scheme that organizes the facts of a situation.*

This is an approach for testing ideas with people who like theories, data, and solving puzzles. Problem solvers with new or poorly structured questions can use this tool to clarify the major variables, constraints, and opportunities. Working silently intentionally slows the process, allowing each member to play with ideas for classification that might be lost if the group were dominated by a vocal idea leader.

OUTCOMES: *An explanation or theory of the situation and a rationale for solving the problem.*

1. Randomly list all relevant data, facts, and aspects of the situation on a large board or flip chart. Use brief noun-verb phrases and sentences to describe your ideas.

SAMPLE USES:

• *A wholesaler regrouping large numbers of products to get clearer management control.*

• *An ecology group trying to improve their organization of waste and pollution sources.*

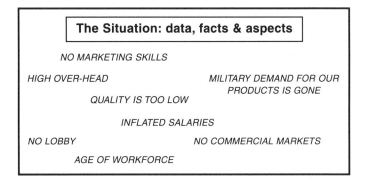

2. Transfer each item to a card or adhesive note and randomly post them on a board or lay them out on the floor.

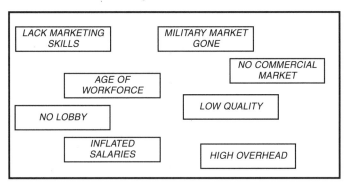

3. Sort the cards, looking for affinities or relations among groups of items. Work silently as a group.
   • Sort by impression, feelings, and gut reaction.
   • Duplicate cards that belong in two or more groupings.
   • Work silently to aid participation and unconventional thinking.
   • Some cards may end up by themselves without a group.

4. Arrange the cards in columns of like groupings. Create a header card for each column. Use a concise phrase that captures the essence of the group of cards. Think of the header card as a news headline that tells the story of the column or as a topical sentence for a paragraph which contains the data.

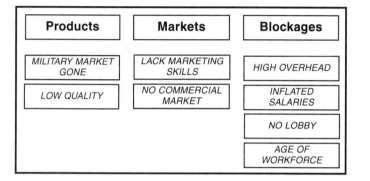

Products	Markets	Blockages
MILITARY MARKET GONE	LACK MARKETING SKILLS	HIGH OVERHEAD
LOW QUALITY	NO COMMERCIAL MARKET	INFLATED SALARIES
		NO LOBBY
		AGE OF WORKFORCE

5. Using the header topics as a guide, search for a theory or model that will explain the data. Use any personal experience you have with classification systems or consult reference books for models. Examples you might use could be:

- Stages of company development
- The "seven S's of strategy"
- Marketing Mix
- An analogy, perhaps to cooking

6. Test the results.

- Is the theory supported by new facts?
- Does it produce new insights?
- Does it get beyond ways of classifying that led to the problem?

7. Write down a statement of the theory or insights that you will use to identify a solution:

"Fair participation requires openness, free data distribution, and competence."

TEST

GROUP SIZE: *Fewer than 12 people. Break into subgroups for larger groups.*

TIME REQUIREMENTS: *2-4 hours for all but the most trivial issues.*

SPACE FACILITIES: *Open space to display and sort cards is critical.*

EQUIPMENT: *A flat wall space, tack board, or two flip charts.*

DATA: *It is better not to collect data in advance–it tends to bias the search. Have data accessible as theories and ideas are brought forward for testing.*

REFERENCES:
Brassard, M. (1989).
Kawakito, Jiro; see Mizuno, S. (1988).

TEST

PURPOSE: *To test the comparative strengths of opposing designs. Sharpen arguments favoring each extreme to uncover deep flaws and provide insight.*

OUTCOMES: *A resolution of arguments between proponents of extreme positions that provides ideas for going beyond the conflict.*

SAMPLE USES:

• *Major transitions such as plant closings.*

• *Setting direction for research efforts or major marketing strategies.*

• *Serious diplomatic questions where there are corporate, world-wide, or global consequences.*

RECONCILING DILEMMAS

The dilemmas of organizational life and commerce are seldom resolved but are momentarily put on hold by some rephrasing or accommodation. This tool is aimed at issues that are reworked again and again such as economies of scale vs. flexibility, centralization vs. decentralization, tough-mindedness vs. responsiveness. It is the epitome of a testing tool; however it is not an easy tool to use. Like many cures, it has side effects. It may alienate those whose solutions are not accepted.

1. **Form a sharpened image of the opposing points:**

    • Eliminate the moderate views from both sides.

    • Identify 2-5 of the strongest proponents of each extreme.

    • Build issue characterizations that are the two most extreme, while still being manageable.

    • Have a leader or facilitator review the positions, insuring that they are truly extreme.

◄── POLARIZE ──►

2. **Solve the problem from each extreme:**

    • Select groups of 5-15 people to advocate each extreme position.

    • Have each group solve the problem completely from their extreme.

    • Then, have each group argue against the effectiveness of the other extreme.

3. Form a synthesis between the two extremes:

- Have each of the two extreme groups present their arguments and counter-arguments to a third group whose members have no affiliation with the extremes.

- The third group's task is to find a synthesis between the two extreme groups.

- Have the third group present their synthesis to the entire group and the leader for testing and approval.

- Have the entire group refine the synthesis, taking into account the critique.

- The leader's task is to bring everyone into accord. Care needs to be taken to soften negative feelings that may have arisen in the sharply opposed positions.

TEST

GROUP SIZE: *This exercise requires a large commitment, perhaps 24 people working over 1-2 days. The original formulation and data preparation calls for 5-7 staff members.*

TIME REQUIREMENTS:

Position preparation can take considerable staff time, but the event itself is a one day plus exercise. Do it preferably over one evening and the following day. Follow-up continues indefinitely.

PREPARATION: *Extensive data collection to set extreme positions accurately.*

REFERENCES:

Hampton-Turner, C. (1990). Mason, R & Mitroff, I. (1981). McWhinney W. (1992).

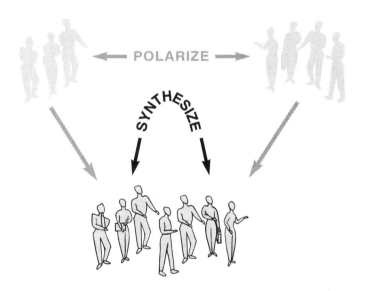

POLARIZE

SYNTHESIZE

4. On-going testing of the solution.

A true synthesis, or even a compromise, may induce untried ideas. Following implementation, you need to continually review the process to anticipate troubles. A testing program uses the strategy of going back and forth between extremes positions to determine the best operating region. This testing establishes ranges beyond which the extreme strategies are deemed unwise to pursue. Such extreme positions might result in employee loss or prohibitive health costs. The limits on extreme positions prevent damage while searching for a long-term solution.

TEST

SWOTS

PURPOSE: *To test existing and planned strategies against internal Strengths and Weaknesses, and external Opportunities and Threats— "SWOTS"—determining which plan works best.*

OUTCOMES: *A risk analysis of strategies and some redesigns that lead to the selection of the best strategies.*

COMMENTS: *This is an exercise of Sensory awareness. It looks at the opportunities and constraints that face an organization when implementing an existing or potential path. It directs a group to look at the worst and best outcomes. By setting the Internal and External groups to test each other, the process accents the tensions that surround any action.*

SAMPLE USES:
• *Entering new markets and new distribution systems.*

• *Establishing new social policies and regulations.*

• *Working in arenas with which the management is relatively unfamiliar with the situation.*

1. **Divide your group into two working sub-groups:**
   • *"Internal"* to identify *Strengths* and *Weaknesses* of the operation: operating divisions, staff, finance, auditing, and research.

   • *"External"* to identify *Opportunities* and *Threats* in the marketplace: marketing, consumer relations, buyers, technical intelligence, board members, customers, and suppliers.

2. **Have each sub-group:**
   • Specify the present or proposed strategy: lay out all the major assumptions, the steps to accomplishing the goals, and the present conditions.

   • Separate and collect all data they can collect within and outside the company, including "bench-marking" with other firms' operations and exploring of new opportunities.

3. **Organize and present the collected data.**
   • List *Strengths, Weaknesses, Opportunities*, and *Threats*, "SWOTs," uncovered in explorations on four separate lists.

   • Summarize the four lists on flip charts. Hang the *Internal Strengths* and *Weaknesses* on one wall in the corner of a room. Hang the *External Opportunities* and *Threats* on the adjoining wall. This arrangement facilitates confrontations of the *Internal* and *External* factors.

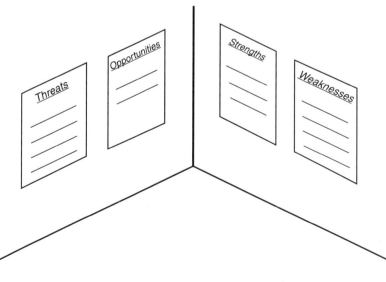

4. Analysis and Testing.

Test each strategy and its elements against each of the SWOT conditions. Identify the impact of the *Internal* and *External* conditions on each strategy by answering the following questions:

	Internal Strengths	**Internal Weaknesses**
External Opportunities	WHAT STRATEGIES WOULD MAKE BEST USE OF OUR STRENGTH IN THE LIGHT OF THE OPPORTUNITIES?	WHAT STRATEGIES WOULD ALLOW US TO TAKE ADVANTAGE OF OPPORTUNITIES IN SPITE OF OUR WEAKNESSES?
External Threats	WHAT STRATEGIES WOULD USE OUR STRENGTHS TO OFFSET THE THREATS?	WHAT STRATEGIES ALLOW US TO MINIMIZE THE THREATS IN SPITE OF OUR WEAKNESSES?

5. Propose strategies.

Have the *Internal* and *External* teams take turns making proposals for evaluating the strategy while the other team challenges those proposals. Working the tensions produces estimations of how likely the plan is to succeed.

6. Select strategies.

Construct a large chart like the one above, leaving room for lists of proposed strategies below each of the four questions. Place the chart on a wall or flip chart. Place each proposed strategy in one of the four boxes where it seems to belong.

Note that the two shaded boxes above contain the most constructive proposed strategies where you *maximize* Strengths and Opportunities and *minimize* Weaknesses and Threats. Strategies within the white boxes have elements that will remain in tension and lead to failures. Any redesign to reduce tensions will improve the potential value of a strategy.

7. Test against established strategies.

Test the results against established strategies to determine which needs to be modified to fit the situation.

 TEST

GROUP SIZE: *The preparation of the data can be done by any set of people. The later four stages use two groups of a dozen or fewer people each.*

TIME REQUIREMENTS: *Major studies can take weeks, but excessively long studies weaken effectiveness.*

PREPARATION: *Extensive when collecting SWOTs data*

REFERENCES:
Weihrich, H. (1982).
Nutt, P. C. & Backoff, W. (1993).

THE ASSERTIVE MODE

The Assertive Mode is based on personal authority, establishing truth or interpreting existing systems of beliefs. It depends on either a charismatic leader or an agent of authority to separate the acceptable from the unacceptable, replace confusion with clarity, or establish rules of conduct and eliminate problem behavior. The play is on the Second Board, where personal power is used to establish strategies and rules that create advantages. The Directional Methods of the Assertive Mode are to Establish and Inspire. Individuals with a "visionary" group leadership style will tend to cycle between Establishing and Inspiring as their preferred approach to planning, resolving conflict, and affecting change.

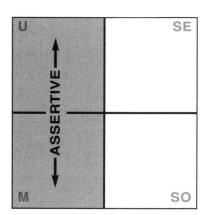

DIRECTIONAL METHODS

ESTABLISH

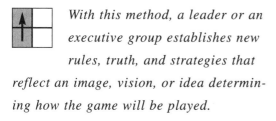 *With this method, a leader or an executive group establishes new rules, truth, and strategies that reflect an image, vision, or idea determining how the game will be played.*

INSPIRE

Inspiring gives expression to a core theme, image, or program that represents a single, true position. It sends a clear message to members of an organization or community.

TOOL	*PAGE*	*TOOL*	*PAGE*
Naming	*138*	*Energizing Policies*	*144*
New Rules	*140*	*Reduced Instruction Set*	*146*
Visioning	*142*		

ESTABLISH

NAMING

PURPOSE: *To name an organization, project or community, and in doing so, define its purpose.*

OUTCOMES: *A name and a corresponding list of expectations, describing what the organization will be to its expected stakeholders.*

COMMENT: *Note that this exercise does not start with a presumption of a clear purpose or function. It often happens that this tool clarifies these concepts so we suggest you do not lock in the statement of purpose prematurely.*

SAMPLE USES:

• *Naming a new firm and setting purpose.*

• *Renaming a merged pair of enterprises.*

• *Naming a project while clarifying its task.*

• *Visioning, to get a feeling of what it would be like "to be called by a different name."*

Naming is a critical and powerful step in creating a new organization. It strongly controls a group's destiny. A name focuses the energy both in and around the entity. If the name and the intent are at odds, the focus is diffused. This tool is a projective instrument, identifying what image the founders want the stakeholders to get from the name.

1. What do you want your company name to say?

List the major stakeholders. A typical list will include one to two dozen people. Identify the relationship of yourself and the stakeholders to the organization. If you are doing the exercise alone, work in a notebook. If two or more members are involved build a list on a flip chart.

2. Create stakeholder "pseudo-quotes."

Imagine how the stakeholders would respond to the organization's name. What would they think? How would it make them feel? Enter the stakeholder's name and a corresponding "pseudo-quote" (see page 152) on a chart. Include your own name and a quote about what you would like the name to say.

STAKE-HOLDER	PSEUDO-QUOTE
_____	_____
_____	_____
_____	_____
_____	_____
_____	_____
_____	_____

3. Identify themes.

When you have created pseudo quotes for everyone, look for themes and appearances that surprise you. Collect these themes on a new sheet to rework. Formulate a summary statement in any natural form.

4. Match the pseudo-quotes to the Realities.

Consider each pseudo-quote, theme, and summary statement. Identify the dominant Reality within which each quote is formed. Make a large Reality chart. Write each quote in the appropriate quadrant. Does the chart match the dominant Realities of your founding members? If not you may have problems.

UNITARY QUOTES	SENSORY QUOTES
_____	_____
_____	_____
_____	_____
MYTHIC QUOTES	**SOCIAL QUOTES**
_____	_____
_____	_____
_____	_____

5.   What the names say.

Consider the image and focus of names developed from each Reality. The following statements summarize what a company name *says* coming from each Reality.

UNITARY:	This is your territory.
SENSORY:	Historical or place associations that are significant to you.
SOCIAL:	The Function or purpose.
MYTHIC:	Evoke a metaphor or Mythic character you identify with.

6.   Names and the Realities.

Display a Reality chart with examples of company names arranged according to the four quadrant Reality structure. Work with some examples to make sure that everyone understands. Brainstorm potential company names without judgement. Place each name into one of the four quadrants where it belongs.

UNITARY	SENSORY
"AMERICAN STRATEGY CENTER"	"THE BRIDGER HOUSE"
"CHIRON, INC."	"NEW PARADIGM CONSULTING, INC."
MYTHIC	**SOCIAL**

7.   Choose a name.

When you have generated three or more potential company names in each quadrant, test them against the values of the group. Refer to the themes and summary statement generated in step 3.

- Introduce other constraints such as: names already in use, undesirable acronyms, legal restrictions, etc.

- Formulate the summary statement in a way that fits the name.

- Selection of a name usually should be a unanimous choice among those involved. Leave time and emotional space to resolve doubts

8.   An Example name:

"The Bridger House, *Entrepreneurial Leadership in the Service of a Community.*"

This example uses the name of a great pioneer to indicate the action orientation of a Mythic-Sensory founders group.

ESTABLISH

GROUP SIZE: *2 people or a small group.*

TIME REQUIREMENTS: *Minimum of one hour, but typically 2-3 hours for a small group. Ideal for an evening meeting with follow-up the next morning. Do not rush the acceptance of a name. It is hard to recover from a bad naming.*

PREPARATION: *All participants should have familiarity with the four Realities.*

EQUIPMENT: *Flip chart or large sheets on the wall.*

DATA: *It may be helpful to have a directory of names that are already used by other companies or institutions.*

ESTABLISH

NEW RULES

This is a good technique to use when you are exploring the implications of a new policy or administrative rule. It establishes the new policy or rule within the existing structure, assuring its acceptance, and is the epitome of Second Board play.

PURPOSE: *To establish rules, policies, and strategies that reflect an image or idea, determining how the game is played.*

OUTCOMES: *A set of rules, strategies, or policies to implement an idea or image.*

SAMPLE USES:

• *New or changing policies, strategies, or rules.*

OPTION #1 ESTABLISHING NEW RULES
(When no prior rules exist.)

1. **Write** a statement identifying the idea, image, or vision to be established.

2. **Brainstorm** a list of new rules, policies, and strategies that reflect the idea or image. Use your personal experience and knowledge of formats applicable to the situation, such as goals, objectives, strategies, or policies.

> NEW RULES, POLICIES & STRATEGIES
> _____
> _____
> _____
> _____
> _____

3. **Select** from the list the most appropriate rules, truths, or strategies. Look at the list, editing ideas as necessary (refine, rewrite, rearrange, eliminate, add to).

4. **Establish** a final list of rules, truths, or strategies.

OPTION #2 CHANGING EXISTING RULES

ESTABLISH

1. Write a statement identifying the idea, image or vision to be established.

2. Create and detail the ideal characteristics of this image ignoring any potential constraints or concerns.

3. Compare the ideal image with the actual situation, identifying the gaps between the two. Notice the analysis of the actual situation is often available from a prior step in your Path of Change.

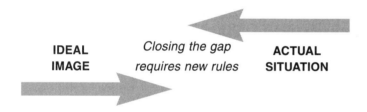

IDEAL IMAGE   *Closing the gap requires new rules*   **ACTUAL SITUATION**

4. Brainstorm a list of new rules, policies, and strategies that would make the ideal possible. Assert Mythic ideas that override current Unitary policies.

5. Compare the new rules to the old rules. Determine if the new rules are different enough to achieve the idea, image, or vision. Revise the new rules if they are not sufficient.

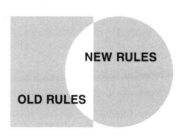

NEW RULES

OLD RULES

6. Establish the rule, truth, or principle in written form for subsequent implementation design. Remove old rules that impede achievement of the idea.

GROUP SIZE: *3-9 people. When working with large groups, break into sub-groups of 5-7 people.*

TIME REQUIREMENTS: *Approximately 4 hours.*

SPACE FACILITIES: *A class or conference room.*

PREPARATION: *Copies of Instructions with examples. Work from copies of any pre-existing rules, strategies, or policies.*

EQUIPMENT: *Flip chart, markers, access to copier, overhead and transparencies.*

REFERENCES: *Webber, J. (1991).*

ESTABLISH

VISIONING

Visioning creates a *Renaissance* image of the company for the executives to proclaim throughout the organization.

PURPOSE: *To create a belief and a following for an established ideal, economic program, way of doing business, or a political stance within a group.*

OUTCOMES: *A rich and enticing image of what can be expected from following a leadership or creed.*

COMMENT: *This is one of four tools for creating images of change. The other three are:*

Metaphors: A device used to reframe a problem, develop fresh, enticing ideas.

Story-Telling: A tool to influence a group to adopt a position through expressing emotions, feelings, fears, and empathy.

Future Perfect: A method of giving courage through focusing on the "destined" future.

SAMPLE USES:
- *To develop energy behind a corporate direction.*

- *To sell a new program or thrust (e.g. "re-engineering").*

- *To organize a crusade.*

1. Prepare the Vision.

The vision itself is prepared by a creative individual or team, using one or more of the following:

- A study, sometimes extensive, of the program or system to be visioned. From this, the team extracts the core values and purposes, using the *Story Telling* or *Metaphor* tools, on pages 168 and 178, with the program executives.

- An exploration, sometimes intensive, looking for the unconscious motivations, fears, and aspirations for where the organization should focus its energies.

- A cultural survey for heroes, songs, cinema, happenings, or places of sentiment which link the member's heritage to the program's intent.

- Creation of an elegant core image, a metaphor, on which to organize a campaign. Often the metaphor is a journey, "getting on board with..." expressing a sub-culture's myth.

- A program (often one in popular usage such as TQM) that the executives wish to adopt.

2. Campaign to Proclaim the Vision.

The effort to establish a vision as a vehicle for a belief or principle can range from a simple posting of a notice to an elaborate national crusade such as those that have swept China in recent decades.

3. Maximum Participation.

Acceptance may come from participation by the membership in developing the idea. Here, the leaders present the idea as a seed to be developed, one that is not viable without the generative involvement of the members. The metaphoric image is presented as an organic, living image to be grown in the process of organic adoption. This is a participative campaign that forms a contagion of enlarging circles or participation or local initiatives. Guidance (control) is accomplished through periodic ritualized "reporting" of initiatives and accomplishments.

4. An Example:

An elegant example is reported by Marjorie Parker who used a metaphor of a garden to drive the rebirth of an aluminum smelter town in Norway. Every element of the town became a plot in a vast "garden" designed and tended by the worker-citizens. The illustration is the core drawing of a plant conceived as a whole garden. Many more "gardens" were drawn by the employees and citizens of the community. The metaphor was "proclaimed" in recreating the entire plant and town.

What the Garden Symbolizes:

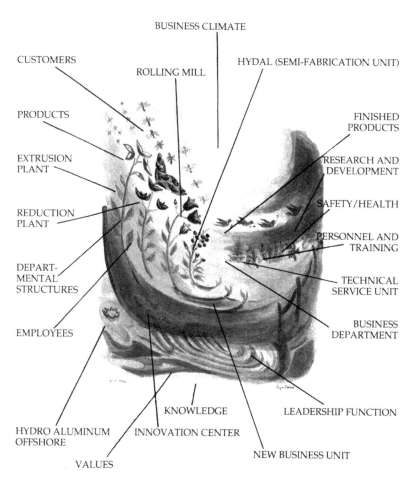

ESTABLISH

GROUP SIZE: *Not relevant since a team does the visioning which is imprinted into a population of any size.*

TIME REQUIREMENTS: *Variable with the importance of the task. It could take months to mount a campaign.*

PREPARATION: *A major part of the task. Preparation can be extensive and expensive.*

EQUIPMENT: *From a megaphone to full multi-media extravaganzas.*

DATA: *Data on the image and resources and attitudes of the members may need to be conveyed.*

REFERENCES: *Parker, M. (1990).*

INSPIRE

ENERGIZING POLICIES

This tool is the instillation of a principle as a grand idea. Everyone unconditionally follows the charismatic leader.

PURPOSE: *To create a core theme, or image that represents a focused position based on a set of policies, rules, and principles. To reconcile discrepancies to form a fresh, new program mobilizing energy.*

OUTCOMES: *A program that reconciles discrepancies or represents a collection of truths or rules.*

SAMPLE USES:

• *For any discrepancies in under standing policy or principles.*

• *Developing new principles or rules for programs.*

• *Need new ideas or programs.*

1. Identify.

Identify and list the established policies, rules, and principles from the Unitary Reality that will be interpreted or reinterpreted.

2. Personalize.

Develop a personal interpretation of the policies, rules, and principles by filling in the missing words in the following statements.

"As I see.......it means......."

"The way I feel about.......is......."

"I envision.......as......."

"I experienced.......to be......."

For example: The following sentences represent how a manager responded to a set of policies for growth and expansion of services.

"As I see *growth* it means *more opportunities.*"

"The way I feel about *expansion* is *that it could dilute our efforts and reputation.*"

"I envision *growth* as a *bustling city.*"

"I experience *growth* to be *exhilarating and powerful.*"

3. Group.

Uncover themes within the personal interpretations. Group similar items in a column and develop a header card for each column.

HEADER CARD	*HEADER CARD*	*HEADER CARD*	*HEADER CARD*

4. Convert the language.

Convert the policy language into images, slogans, and games. These are most effective when created by those involved in carrying out the policies. They also can be done by public relations specialists.

5. Present the images.

These converted images are then presented to management with whatever means necessary to gain commitment and energy for carrying out the policy work.

6. Develop a campaign.

One way is to transform the policies into heroic visualizations on which to focus celebration of concurrence.

- For example, the consultant Jim Channon creates large dynamic motivational pictures which present the corporate strategies as crusades and epic *strikes* against the *enemies* of corporate effectiveness. These presented in highly ritualized setting embolden the managers to take on demanding assignments.

7. Inspire.

The visualization presentation of the policies inspires commitment without giving openings to discussion of details or implications.

INSPIRE

GROUP SIZE: *An entire team or corporate management.*

TIME REQUIREMENTS: *2-4 hours.*

SPACE FACILITIES: *Conference room or auditorium..*

PREPARATION: *From simply a good understanding of the beliefs to be addressed, up to a full multimedia presentation.*

EQUIPMENT: *Flip charts, marker, paper, and pencils.*

INSPIRE

PURPOSE: *To articulate an idea as a clear workable model for implementation.*

OUTCOMES: *Preparation of an idea for acceptance.*

SAMPLE USES:

• *Revitalizing an existing flow diagram or model.*

SIMPLE MODELING

This is a tool for achieving a clear model of a process by keeping the description of the process and the related problems clear and simple. It is part of the larger method called "soft systems methodology" from Peter Checkland. It leads directly to feasible plans and a clarity that helps gain acceptance for an initiative. The restriction to a small number of phrases is critical to achieving this clarity.

The *Simple Modeling* process expands a statement of the objective into a series of simple statements. Each statement is formed by an action *Verb* and an object or event called a *State*, where the *Verb* is doing something to the *State*. Examples would be, "assemble packages," "call home," and "remove garbage." Do not use phrases like "Improve morale," since morale is a condition, not an object or event. Here we follow Checkland's process in designing a flow process.

1.   The root diagram.

A "root diagram" depicts the desired solution. The figure below shows the root diagram for a publishing operation:

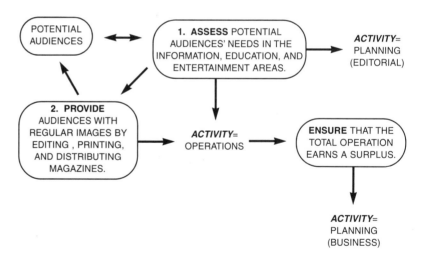

2.   Build your own "root diagram."

From this basic model you lay out the process by forming a network of *Verb/State* phrases such as "assess audience," "assemble material," and "edit copy." These phrases can be written on large Post-its and placed along a network of paths from *Start* to *Finish* drawn on a large wall chart. They can be written and posted either by individuals or collectively. Ideally, each person will produce 5-12 verb phrases.

3. Culling, organizing, and connecting.

Edit the cards, culling duplicates and improperly formed phrases. Organize the cards in the flow paths, notice gaps where steps have been omitted, and where there are inconsistencies in the levels of action. Connect everything with arrows that show the sequences and dependencies.

4. Review and reform.

With each culling you may find you need to reorganize the paths, change the boundaries of the processes, set new levels of detail in the descriptions and go back to writing more *Verb/State* cards.

5. Outcome.

The outcome is a flow chart showing the boundaries, actions, and flows of the desired process.

6. Example: An Operational System.

The figure below is a publishing example of an operational system. It can be expanded indefinitely as the design is fully implemented.

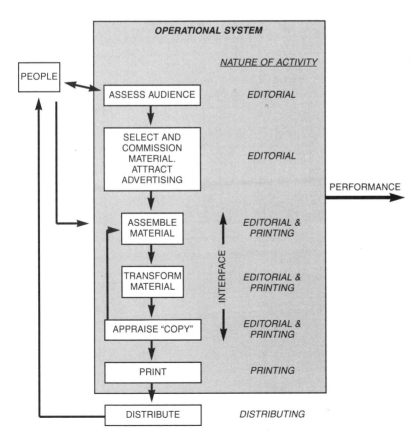

 INSPIRE

GROUP SIZE: *A small group representing a breadth of viewpoints.*

TIME REQUIREMENTS: *Highly variable. It is best to do the tool in two or more sessions, allowing reflection and perspective to be gained.*

SPACE FACILITIES: *Conference room with open wall space for posting the cards and the full model.*

PREPARATION: *If the work is a redesign, a physical walk through the process in advance will provide a motor awareness of the function.*

DATA: *Introduce detailed measures and technical data at the next stage in which the model is reduced to a design.*

REFERENCES: *Checkland, P. (1989).*

THE INFLUENTIAL MODE

The Influential Mode is based on the preferences people hold, by either changing or establishing those preferences. It depends on the interplay between values and principles to change moral and ethical positions and values. It imposes truth by authority or establishes new rules of behavior from the value position of individuals. The play is on the Third Board, where power, politics, and strategy are used to create an operational advantage. Change affects belief systems that are founded in habits, needs, fears, and expectations. Change also affects the inclusion and exclusion of members and their responsibilities. The Influential Mode uses the two Directional Method, to Persuade and Convert. Individuals with a consultative group leadership style will tend to cycle between Persuading and Converting as their preferred approach to planning, resolving conflict, and affecting change.

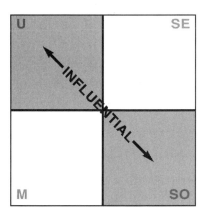

DIRECTIONAL METHODS

PERSUADE

This method introduces new rules and changes existing rules to instill the values of a group into a broader community.

CONVERT

This method converts others to established world views or principles, changing their preferences and values to beliefs.

PERSUADE

PURPOSE: *To form a consensus on which to base policies, group operations, or plans. Useful particularly when disagreements have already surfaced in the group.*

OUTCOMES: *A charter of understanding about what values the group shares and procedures for dealing with conflicts.*

SAMPLE USES:

• *Reducing open conflict in a group.*

• *The merging of groups that have different histories and disciplines.*

• *Surfacing of hidden difficulties in a group that is not performing effectively.*

BEYOND DISRUPTION

This process is built on the idea that an organization's policies, rules, and plans will be carried out most effectively if the participants share common values and intents. Otherwise, conflicts tend to surface with every new demand from the environment. The group forms a consensus, getting into each other's heads to develop shared values. It is a "left-brain" exercise.

The tool is straight forward and avoids hard to handle emotional issues. It is containable and has definite outcomes. The product is immediately useful to the group and to the parent organization.

1. Coming together, time to pause and clear your head.

Settle the group; ask everyone to "dump" their present concerns about the situation onto individual sheets of paper. The list should include personal feelings, gripes, group problems, and larger issues. This list is not to be shared. Each person scans their list for issues that need to be worked in the group if they are to be satisfied. Then, they divide their list into two separate lists. The "A" list consists of group issues they need to work on to be satisfied. The "B" list consists of personal concerns they choose not to share. Have everyone put these personal "B" lists away.

Working from their individual "A" lists, have the group compose a joint problem list. A moderator can help organize and simplify the list. Without a moderator it is best to leave the items as they were presented. Trying to simplify allows group members to quibble over details and consequently avoid the real task.

2. Becoming aware.

Organize into groups of people who are in general agreement on the issue. Move to separate rooms or far enough apart for privacy. In groups or individually write out statements of how each problem can be solved, listing the needed processes, and desired outcomes. Work for consensus within the groups, noting disagreements within the group. The effort should not be hurried, better solutions produce better outcomes. Take care not to run over any individual's feelings.

Take a long break and return to the same sub-groupings. Reflect on the solutions. Take a point of view you believe any opposing group would have to your suggestions. Mark every element of your solutions with which you sense the others would not agree.

3. Form two lists on a flip chart.

- Solutions you think everyone will agree with and accept.
- Solutions you think others will not accept, pointing out what values are in conflict with yours.

This is a critical step in the use of this tool. You may insult the others if you treat it casually.

4. Compare values and images.

Each group or individual presents their lists to the total group. Go through your lists point by point, coming to a consensus about which solutions should be on the "accepted" and "not accepted" lists. Coming to an understanding and appreciation of other's values is key to the discussion. Agreement is not required, only an open sharing of values, tolerance, and respect.

New issues are likely to surface during this process. Frequently, they are issues on people's personal "B" lists, where issues are sensitive and strong value differences are found.

5. Reformulate solutions.

Return to the sub-groupings and reformulate solutions to fit the new value expressions. Wherever there remain areas in contention, write a procedure for working them via a compromise.

6. Share.

Get the group back together, sharing solutions and working out agreements on the procedure for handling future disagreements.

Attend to the new issues that are coming up, many will be attempts to avoid closure on new power alignments. These avoidances should be worked through.

7. Write a statement.

Write up a shared statement of the group product:
- A group Charter with operating rules for resolving conflict.
- A Logo with a "Bill of Agreements."
- Create a Mythic tale about the group getting its act together. Creating this tale is an excellent event for a session following an evening meal. This is an empowering way to bond the group around their resolution. It might come from using the *Future Perfect* tool on page 184 to close the session.

 PERSUADE

GROUP SIZE: *Break groups of more than 24 into sub-groups. If there are more than 2 sub-groups it is best to have one or more facilitators to support openness and contain contention.*

TIME REQUIREMENTS: *This is an all day exercise. It is best concluded with a supper and evening closing session.*

SPACE FACILITIES: *Separate break out rooms for each group. If working as individuals, a room with capacity three times the number of participants.*

PREPARATION: *If conflicts are deep, a premeeting to discuss the process separately within sub-groups.*

EQUIPMENT: *A flip chart for each group.*

REFERENCES:
Gemmill, G & Costello (1990). Johnson, L (1991).

PERSUADE

PURPOSE: *Publicly to share values a group holds. To develop a mission or plan, or to instill a value, image, or culture in a group. The tool is used to build consensus.*

OUTCOMES: *A set of images and attached values that display the principles held by a group, particularly in a form that indicates how the group wishes to be seen by other groups or by the public.*

SAMPLE USES:

• *Culture setting at the beginning of a new project.*

• *Bonding for a newly formed diverse group.*

• *Morale building after a difficult event.*

PSEUDO-QUOTES

This is an emotionally supportive exercise through which the group gets a sense of shared values without having to go through the issues of prioritizing or voting for preferences. It can be used to form a cultural image, to identify what the group stands for. It identifies the kind of ceremony and the types of people the group values. It can also be used to reinforce the values by being repeated within an organization, with subsequent groups adding their images, stories, and values to the initial picture. The imaging can be used repeatedly to express a continuously adaptive cultural consensus.

1. **The process.**

Prepare an event, a *testimonial*, on the occasion of a great achievement of the organization, community, or person. Have the group fantasize their participation. For example, a number of people coming to celebrate the event and telling what they think of your achievement and you as a person. They describe what meaning the occasion has for them.

2. **The group forms a fantasy of the occasion, imagine.**

• The specific achievement that is being celebrated.

• The place and form of celebration.

• Some examples of the guest who would be honoring you.

3. **Working individually, each person:**

• Makes a list of the people they would have come to the celebration. (They can be real people in your life, prominent figures, fictional people, or historical figures.)

• Makes up a phrase or sentence in the form of a quote that each guest would ideally say, supporting you and your achievement. If is essential that these be stated as direct quotes to assure an authentic feeling.

4. **Divide into groups of 2-4 people.**

Identify the values behind the quotes. Get at what the person valued in having the "guest" say the words he or she put in their mouths. Talking from within the fantasized occasion will help the individual stay in touch with the feelings.

5. Work to collect the characteristic quotes.

The values and related stories are collected and reproduced on a common display. This can be done by each person picking one or a few of their favorite sources and quotes to add to the whole. The output is a figure such as one created by a Public TV station showing the source, the quote, and the implied value.

6. The image forms a base on which to build.

Once the figure has been assembled, the next step might be to direct a change in the culture, organize values on which to build policies, indoctrinate new members, or open opportunities that arise from newly valued ideas.

PSEUDO-QUOTES FROM A PUBLIC TV STATION:

PERSUADE

GROUP SIZE: *The minimum that will give a semblance of the fantasized occasion.*

TIME REQUIREMENTS: *One hour, but the quality will be better if you take 2 hours.*

SPACE FACILITIES: *A wall space for display.*

EQUIPMENT: *A roll of "butcher paper" and props for the celebration.*

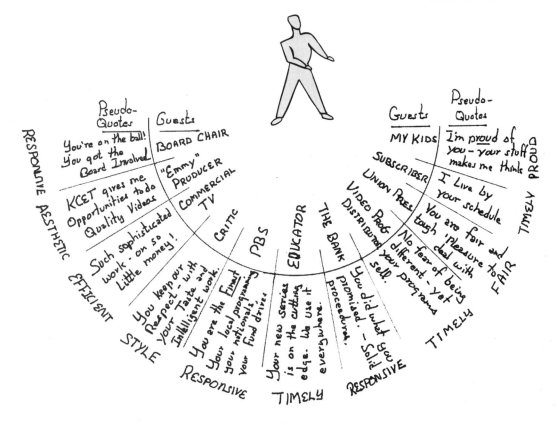

PERSUADE

PURPOSE: To work through a conflict, simulating a conversation in which you observe your own attitudes and arguments. It prepares those involved for the actual engagement sometimes eliminating conflict by exploring one's own position.

OUTCOMES: A clarification of the issue where the conversation points toward resolution or prepares, positions, or trains you for an actual confrontation.

SAMPLE USES:

• *Preparation for an interorganizational or interpersonal negotiation.*

• *Uncovering hidden motivations and feelings that interfere with achieving a solution.*

• *Building a selling "pitch."*

VALUE SYNERGIZING

This tool makes you aware of your entanglements in a conflict. Systematically talking through a problem with observers often leads to a "way out." It clarifies the question so emotional issues do not cloud the exchange, heading off conflicts before they occur. It uses simulation to improve awareness of the sources of issues inside you and your organization.

1. **Find a phrase that summarizes the conflict at hand.** Enter it in the center of a circle. Identify 5-8 major stakeholders that your group must confront to resolve the problem. Enter their names in a segment of the perimeter.

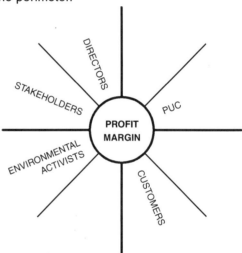

2. **Set up the scene for a simulated conversation.** Select a person who is to talk with a stakeholder who is critical to the conflict.

3. **Organize a chart**, as diagrammed on the following page, on a sheet of paper about 8 feet long. Post it on a wall or drawing board. Hold a simulated conversation with the involved members from your group, having them answer the following questions:

    • What did *they* say, to start the conversation (first sentence)?

    • What do you say in response?

    • What is your reason for your response?

    • What are your emotions behind your reason?

    • What do you believe are their reasons and emotions? (Your view of them is clearer after exploring your own emotions.)

4. Example: The Public Utility Commission (PUC) is blocking a hike in the rate for service.

PERSUADE

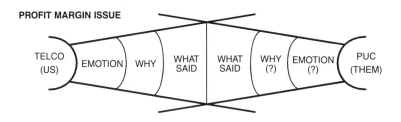

PROFIT MARGIN ISSUE

TELCO (US)			PUC (THEM)	
EMOTION	WHY (Value)	WHAT SAID	WHAT SAID	WHY (Value)
RIGHTEOUS	NEED CAPITAL TO MAINTAIN DIVIDENDS	WE NEED 14% HIKE IN RATES	YOU ARE ALREADY OVER-CHARGING THE PUBLIC	PROTECTING EXPLOITED MASSES

Observers commented that the PUC "value" represented only a few people in the PUC and that many were helpful and understood the needs of businesses. They suggested a second possible way the conversation could start. Thus...

			YOU DON'T KNOW YOUR COSTS— YOU'RE HIDING INEFFICIENCIES	YOU ARE POOR BUSINESSMEN

A second observer noted that a helpful initiation could occur...

			YOU'RE TOO BLATANT IN JUMPING RATES	BE SMART!

Which led to expressing a new value and consequently a new "What Said" to the PUC...

CONNECTING WITH THE CUSTOMERS	OUR BUSINESS IS SERVICE	NEW FACILITIES WILL PROVIDE BETTER SERVICE		

AND SO ON...

GROUP SIZE: *A minimum of 3 people, with one observer. In demonstration format, this can be used to solve an issue with a large audience.*

TIME REQUIREMENTS: *Varies with importance. A major issue might call for several 3 hour sessions to work many scenarios.*

SPACE FACILITIES: *A free wall on which to hang the chart.*

PREPARATION: *The involved people must be well grounded in the issues. Prepare charts in advance.*

EQUIPMENT: *Roll of paper or other large writing surface.*

DATA: *Usually participants will recognize a need for data as arguments unfold.*

REFERENCES: *Argyris, C. (1982).*

This sample led to the group to seeing that many PUC staff members were concerned with good business practices. Thus, the Telco staff would benefit from reviewing their rate proposal arguments.

The path of these discussions can lead to many outcomes, including shifting into an actual open conversation conducted with the same self-reflective method.

CONVERT

PURPOSE: *To get a community of agreement behind a new policy or rule that has been adopted by an organization's leaders or an outside authority.*

OUTCOMES: *A shared positive attitude toward the policy.*

SAMPLE USES:

• *Getting an organization behind a new leader.*

• *Accepting a budgetary restriction.*

• *Installing an employee safety policy.*

GETTING THE MESSAGE

This tool is designed to build a consensus of agreement, a belief in a policy, or a rule or way doing business. In using this tool, the group accepts the policy as a given; the task is to gain acceptance for the policy. Working with the tool gives participants a sense of membership in a community of shared understanding and commitment.

1. Deepen the message.

Choose a small group of 5-9 people from the larger group to form a formal policy statement. For example, a dress code, rules for purchasing agent relations with suppliers, or an affirmative action statement.

Keeping the policy statement in mind, form a more general statement that satisfies the following conditions:

• Does not offend anyone present in the group.

• Does not provide a basis for argument.

• Homogenizes the group's opinions.

• Avoids technicalities that could be tested.

• Leaves people feeling that by conforming to the policy they are socially and politically safe.

• Provides a positive, expansive declaration.

For example, "No personnel decision may be based on the race or sexual preference of an employee." This rule was generalized and made into a positive form as "All personnel decisions will treat employees fairly." The group could settle on a few such statements, as long as the statements do not have overlapping agenda which would leave a basis for arguments.

2. Explain the new statement and the resulting tasks.

Copy the new general statement onto a wall board and arrange the whole group informally around the board. Explain the new policies and principles behind the statement and the resulting tasks.

3. Share experiences or tales.

Divide into sub-groups of 3-5 participants. Encourage each participant to remember an occasion in their work or outside life that illustrates how they or some other person has lived by the new statement. Having a few tales of how someone got in trouble by violating the statement illustrates the message well. The participants should encourage their fellow story tellers. When all participants have spoken within the sub-groups have them select one speaker to share their experience with the entire group.

4. Confirm support.

- Each of the chosen speakers comes to the front of the room, presents their tale, and remains there joined one by one by the other speakers. The facilitator encourages applause and supportive comments.

- If appropriate and time is available have a few more participants come forward and present their tales. It is often effective to have the senior person in the room come forward in support, encouraging by presenting their own story.

- All these acts are intended to build a sense of community that forms around the generalized positive form of the policy statement.

5. Test acceptance.

The community of acceptance will usually be stronger if the sub-groups are formed again and the members share ideas on how they will implement the explicit policy. This strengthens the commitment to supportive action before leaving the meeting.

6. Reinforce the sense of community.

A further step critical to community building action is a meeting of the same people held about a month later in which the prime purpose is to share successes in working within the policy and to help those people who have not "gotten the message."

Note: With some experience in using this tool a facilitator can do the first deepening step with the whole group. This intensification may produce a stronger community concurrence but also can lead to fragmentation and irreconcilable dissent.

CONVERT

GROUP SIZE: *No limitations.*

TIME REQUIREMENTS:
From one hour for the least significant change to a half day.

PREPARATION: *Only "deepening the message" if it is to be done in advance.*

EQUIPMENT: *Best to use an auditorium or other ceremonial space. Do not use an ordinary conference room.*

CONVERT

PURPOSE: *Effectively to gain agreement from a work group on a new organizational policy or structure.*

OUTCOMES: *A positive acceptance of a policy or structure that has been imposed by a management or administrative order.*

SAMPLE USES:

• *New sanitary policies in a dental office.*

• *New expense reporting policy.*

• *Enforcement of immigration regulations.*

SCENARIO

Scenario building is used to convert a doubting group to accepting a new policy or operating reality. *Scenarios* help us explore the impact of policies, strategies, and constraints on a situation and are often used to compare alternative policies.

The group is prepared by getting them to problem solve within the constraints of a policy, rather than attacking it as something threatening. Treat *Scenario* building as if you are working a good riddle.

1. Prepare.

Begin with a tone-setting exercise, directing the energy toward working positively with the imposed constraints. Use an innocent exploration. For example, consider building a house constrained by having to preserve the two trees in the middle of the lot.

Have subgroups of 3-6 people work on the design of such a sample constrained situation for up to an hour. Bring the sub-groups together to discuss the handling of the constraints, building a sense of challenge in working with, not against, the policy constraints.

2. Explore the impact of the contended policy.

• Formulate the new policy as a set of requirements and constraints. Take them as the givens of the *Scenario* exercise. They are the guidelines on which a *Scenario*, an image of a future time, will be constructed.

• Identify what data is necessary to make the policy operation. For example, if a policy is to increase sales by at least 12% the data needed are the dollar amount and the history of responses to prior growth policies. The data should be good enough to predict a plausible future that would follow from the new policy. With such data you have the simplest form of *Scenario*, an image of today.

• Reflect on the issues and opportunities that appear when the data has been worked into the policies. In some cases, simply facing the impact will eliminate the concerns. If so, the policy is accepted and the method has done its job. But if the members continue to be unsure of the new policy, go on to build a full *Scenario*.

3. *Scenario* building

- A *Scenario* is an image of a future situation. It is constructed formally on explicit assumptions about the present situation and specific changes. Clearly state the new policy and other constraints that will be worked into the *Scenario*. Develop the *Scenario* completely to include most features that may become problems in the future.

- Select a time in the future as described by the *Scenario*. Set up teams to do one or more versions of the scenario, assigning tasks to each, building a complete image with physical, economic, social, political, and environmental conditions that would follow from applying the policy. Determine what the outcome might be at an appropriate date in the future, months or years away.

4. When the *Scenario* is completed "experience the outcome."
Examine the projected situation with an appreciative eye, to develop a personal sense of the quality of the outcome in this future time. Examine these conditions for their compatibility, attractiveness, and suitability to various stakeholder.

5. Evaluate the attitude toward the new policy.

- Determine whether or not the *Scenario* has led your group to believe the new policy fits your organization. Openly discuss qualities of the *Scenario*, without any coercion to come to an agreement. Give the participants time to settle with their ideas.

- Reconvene a day to a week later, allowing participants to become clear about their own emerging attitudes. Regroup and work toward a consensus concerning the place of this policy in the future of the organization. If the consensus effort fails, return to *Scenario* building to create a more positive image.

6. Celebrate!
Celebrate the concurrence of a positive image and show appreciation for the effort. Celebrating emphasizes the belief in a positive future.

CONVERT

GROUP SIZE: *Groups ranging from 7-25 people. Since the point is to change beliefs, personal connections are critical.*

TIME REQUIREMENTS: *These can be long efforts, seldom completed in a single session. Participants may take days to settle on new beliefs.*

SPACE FACILITIES: *It may be useful to have some dedicated space for the duration to give significance to the effort.*

PREPARATION: *Leaders and facilitators need to be thoroughly prepared to avoid counter-productive flashbacks.*

EQUIPMENT: *Planning items include computers and simulation software with good graphic capabilities.*

DATA: *All data that is needed to convert the participants.*

REFERENCES:
Cooperrider, D. L. & Srivasta S. (1990).

THE EVALUATIVE MODE

The Evaluative Mode is based on determining or assigning values. It depends on exploration and shared involvement to develop a value consensus, resolves issues, and initiate actions. The play is on the Fourth Board where value is determined. Change impacts the value of actions and the assignment of responsibilities and opportunities to improve. The Evaluative Mode is made up of two Directional Methods, to Value and Allocate. Individuals with a participative leadership style will tend to cycle between Valuating and Allocating as their preferred approach to planning, resolving conflict, and affecting change.

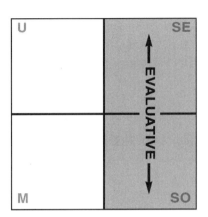

DIRECTIONAL METHODS

VALUE

What matters to us and to others in a situation is the central question of this method. The task is to surface and clarify the values inherent in the situation. The facts or events in a situation are taken as given.

ALLOCATE

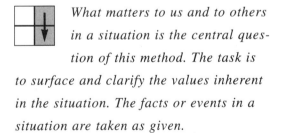

The concern of this method is to chose a fair allocation of resources or to make an assignment or tasks. Shared involvement in allocating ensures a commitment to action. Values are taken as given.

VALUE

PURPOSE: *To open a group to the discussion of difficult issues. Learn a new way to listen, work with different assumptions, and dialogue on issues.*

OUTCOMES: *A readiness to explore and articulate deeply held values, roles, and expectations.*

SAMPLE USES:

A community or organization, preparing for work among people who hold differing world views and who are confronting:

- *Radical changes in economics or technological conditions.*

- *Ethical issues.*

- *Failure of an institution such as the independent status of physicians, acceptance of non-English usage in the workplace, or a corporate takeover.*

DIALOGUE

On any occasion when a group gets to work, they quickly take on roles, speak from long-held assumptions and instinctively defend their opinions. This tool works to stop those habits. It says: *pause, listen,* and *appreciate,* then proceed as *colleagues* on your journey.

This tool enables a group to confront difficult issues, avoiding deadlocks and smoothing inter-group relations for improved effectiveness. It describes the training necessary to work with this mode anywhere along a path. It is best used before any attempts are made to persuade or force decisions.

1. Prepare.

There are two pieces of preliminary work.

- An advance meeting for all participants to learn the purpose and the main differences in Dialogue, discussion, debate, and discourse, and how this knowledge will help them make plans and decisions.

- Presentation about the different world views that are held by members of any group as a way of sharpening their awareness of the depth of differences among themselves. This is done by having the participants take the *Reality Inquiry*, or a world view indicator such as *The Myers-Briggs Type Indicator*, or the *Kolb Learning Style Indicator*. The results are discussed in the group to establish a shared language of differences.

2. Build skills.

- The meetings are explicitly designed to build skills in Dialogue that can help a group do its business and to free the participants from differences created by role or power positions. Thus, everyone sits in one circle (up to about 25 people). Everyone has the same role except for the facilitator who is an outsider to the group.

- The conversation can begin in the general area of concern, but not at a detail level. The purpose is not to solve any problems. It is to become aware of and suspend assumptions and role defenses so that each person can see and reflect on the other's views.

3. Practice skills.

The facilitator provides the group a space in which to practice:

- Listening and speaking without judgement.
- Acknowledging each speaker.
- Respecting and noticing different assumptions and data.
- Suspending roles and status.
- Balancing inquiry and advocacy.
- Focusing on learning.
- Releasing the need for specific outcomes.
- Speaking only when "moved."

4. The flow of Dialogue moves from:

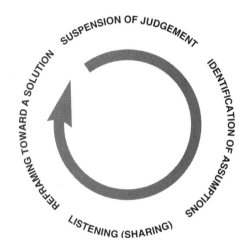

5. Repeat the tool.

The first meeting is ideally a full day to give people a chance to experience "slowing down." Two additional meetings will give most groups a good level of comfort with this tool.

3. Use this tool with other Modes and Methods.

Once learned Dialogue skills can be used everywhere, most especially in the Evaluative, Influential, and Emergent Modes. Any group facing an issue can begin its discussion by warming-up with the eight points listed above. Starting a meeting with practice of Dialogue will increase the likelihood of keeping the discussion to the board on which it most likely is to be resolved.

VALUE

GROUP SIZE: *7 or more people. Divide groups of more than 25 into sub-groups.*

TIME REQUIREMENTS:

Total time for taking and feedback on instrument varies greatly, but each participant typically devotes an hour or so plus sharing time.

First meeting ranges from 2 hours to a more desired full day. Follow-up meetings at intervals of 2-4 weeks need at least 2 hours each.

A dialogue warm-up meeting of 30 minutes should precede the first meeting.

PREPARATION:

Introductory lecture on the process. Skilled presentation and feedback for the Reality Inquiry instrument. Prepare the community to not expect the meetings to produce decisions.

REFERENCES:

Senge, Peter, (1990). (Excellent detailed discussion of this method.)

VALUE

PURPOSE: *To identify the forces that either support or block changes.*

OUTCOMES: *Strategies to diminish restraining forces and strengthen driving forces, enabling change to occur without pockets of resistance.*

COMMENT: *Force Field Analysis was developed by Kurt Lewin in the 1940's to alert us to the blocking power of restraining forces and to focus our attention on the various forces that impede and support a change.*

SAMPLE USES: *Exploration of a problem in a group not skilled in defining and organizing problem-solving activities.*

FORCE FIELD ANALYSIS

This exercise is a basic approach to causal analysis and various derivatives such as the *Causing Effects* tool on page 126.

1. Define the problem.

Working individually, have each person write a brief statement of the problem that the group is to work on. Share these definitions, collecting them on a flip chart, and work them together until a common definition is agreed upon. Write a brief form of this statement in the center of the *Force Field Analysis* diagram, like the one shown below:

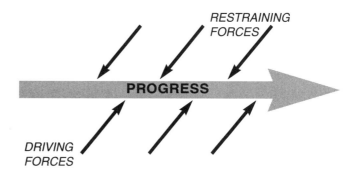

2 . Determine the restraining forces.

Have the group "get into" the problem area, individually visualizing the forces they feel will *interfere* with a solution. Have them write a brief sentence about each force. Collect everyone's ideas, work with the ideas until they are all condensed into a list of about a dozen. List the *restraining* forces on a flip chart.

Test the ideas with the group, making sure they agree each force will interfere with a solution. Eliminate the conditions that are completely unchangeable under the existing circumstances. These items are conditions of the problem, not forces to be worked. Enter the remaining items as Restraining Forces on the *Force Field Analysis* diagram.

3. Determine the driving forces.

Repeat Step #2, looking for the forces that will *contribute* to achieving change. Driving forces are resources of all kinds, new opportunities in the environment, new attitudes, and commitments. Enter these items as *driving forces* on the *Force Field Analysis* diagram. Note that these forces are not solutions themselves, but are part of a solution process.

4. Evaluate both the restraining and driving forces.

Have each person assign an intensity, from one to ten, to each force for its potential to hinder or help solve the issue. Share opinions within the group and come to a consensus on the impact of each force.

5. Develop action plans.

Develop a clear *Action Plan*, see page 124 if you are unfamiliar with this tool, to decide which forces to deal with and which to leave alone. You might begin the change effort with the less intense Restraining forces; efforts there may show immediate success. In selecting the approaches to change take into account the participants' Realities preferences and avoidances reflected on the Reality Matrix.

6. Example: A *Force Field Analysis* diagram.

The following diagram represents an organization that has not been able to improve the skills of its professional employees. The restraining and driving forces have been listed and assigned a numerical value for intensity. Higher numbers represent more pressing issues.

VALUE

GROUP SIZE: *1-12 people.*

TIME REQUIREMENTS: *2 hours to a day, varies with the depth of the issues.*

PREPARATION: *Make Force Field Analysis chart in advance.*

EQUIPMENT: *Wall space for the chart and blank paper.*

REFERENCES: *Lewin, K. (1951).*

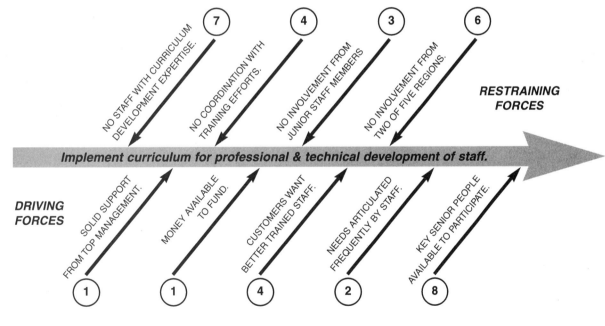

7. Prioritize actions. List the top five actions in order of importance.

FORCE	INTENSITY	ACTION
SENIOR STAFF AVAILABLE	8	SHOW COST-BENEFIT ANALYSIS
NO STAFF EXPERTISE	7	HIRE CURRICULUM DEVELOPMENT CONSULTANT
TWO REGIONS NOT INVOLVED	6	INVITE PARTICIPATION
NO COORDINATION	4	LINK TO OTHER BUDGETS
CUSTOMER COMPLAINTS	4	FEEDBACK MEASURES OF IMPROVEMENT

VALUE

PURPOSE: *To view the scope of an issue and get the stakeholder's values to surface.*

OUTCOMES: *A clear definition of the issue and a list of values important to the stakeholders. Prioritizing values and resolving issues are done by other tools.*

SAMPLE USES:

• *Identifying preferences for employee benefits.*

• *Advising local government on local opinions regarding a new budget.*

STAKEHOLDER WHEEL

This tool is a smaller version of a *Search Conference.* It is used more often in organizational settings when the opportunities are constrained by the organizational objectives.

This version of the search for values is used when the stakeholders or their representatives are present. The *Pseudo-Quotes* tool (page 152) may be used to uncover the values when the stakeholders are absent.

1.   Identify the domain of the issue.

Determine the level at which you will approach the issue. For example, if the *domain* is "Medicine" the *level* could be "Determining the education of a doctor" or "Health care direction in the 21st century." Enter a key term identifying the issue at this level in the center of the *Stakeholder Wheel* below.

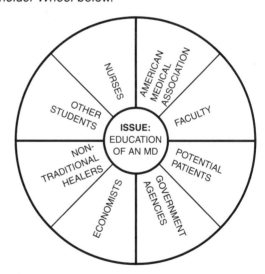

2.   Determine the stakeholders.

Identify up to 12 elements of society who have the greatest stake in this issue. Write their names in the spaces around the central issue of the *Stakeholder Wheel.* Agree upon the list and invite these stakeholders. Inform them that this is a valuing exercise, not a problem solving event.

3. Assemble the various stakeholders. Break into sub-groups of one or more stakeholder categories. Have each group identify a potential program or solution using *Scenario, Visioning,* or *Story Telling* tools (see pages 158, 142, and 168). Inform the stakeholders that their solutions should indicate the types of issues that are important to them. Note that different stakeholders may prefer different imaging techniques according to their dominant Realities.

4. Extract and list the values implied by each sub-group's solution. "What values are implied by our solution?" A powerful way to extract values is by having the stakeholders question the other groups determining their selection and avoidance of particular tasks. A less confrontational method is to have sub-groups extract their own values and present them to the entire group.

5. Simplify and edit the language of the value statements, reframing their original intent. Enter the simplified values onto the *Stakeholder Wheel* as depicted below.

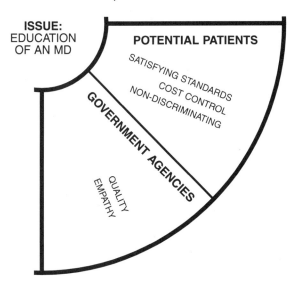

ISSUE:
EDUCATION OF AN MD

POTENTIAL PATIENTS

SATISFYING STANDARDS
COST CONTROL
NON-DISCRIMINATING

GOVERNMENT AGENCIES

QUALITY
EMPATHY

6. Solutions.
These values are now used in the process of designing a solution. Consider how others will react to the values you deem important. To facilitate designing the next step of a Path of Change modify your list to avoid extreme reactions and add explanations where necessary. Note the step of designing a solution is taken with another tool. The *Stakeholder Wheel* identifies *values*, not solutions.

VALUE

GROUP SIZE: *12 or more people. Facilitators are needed with larger group sizes—up to one facilitator for every 12 participants.*

TIME REQUIREMENTS: *One hour for minor issues up to possibly a couple days.*

SPACE FACILITIES: *A room appropriate for 2-3 times the number of participants. Subgroups need audio separation.*

PREPARATION: *Two or more stages of iterative planning to formulate the scope and identify the stakeholders. Care taken in advance pays off handsomely in the outcomes.*

EQUIPMENT: *Flip charts.*

DATA: *Data on stakeholders and issue must be actively sought to insure the proper groups and individuals are involved.*

REFERENCES:
Mason, R. & Mitroff, I. (1981).
Emery, M. (1996).
Morley, D. (1987).
Weisbord, M. (1992).

VALUE

PURPOSE: *The story-based process evokes personal values to support choices of work assignments, reward packages, careers, etc.*

OUTCOMES: *Clear personal or small group priorities. New perceptions of others' attitudes. Alternative possibilities for situations.*

SAMPLE USES:

• *Used at the beginning of a difficult project.*

• *For accepting new workers into an established group.*

• *Used by a group that must write a set of regulations constraining employee activities.*

STORY TELLING

Story Telling offers an initiator a great variety of under-used methods for change. Framing issues through personal expression gives us access to aspects of our minds and emotions unavailable to our linear thinking "left brain." Stories provide a different quality of data— one that is validated by its relation to the whole of a person's life and culture. The process of *Story Telling* reveals the values people hold.

1. **Set the context for *Story Telling*** and give everyone "permission" to explore among their memories. The leader or facilitator may begin by telling a personal story relevant to the issue and then describe how it will be applied to the issue.

2. **Discuss the situation,** opening the topic to assure that people feel free to talk about it from many different approaches. Get the group to agree on a story theme, directing the selection of topics.

For example, in a work assignment problem the theme might be the best stories about work that people remember from childhood. In preparing for a difficult task, the group might explore stories of overcoming hardship in emergencies.

3. **Form into groups** of three or more people and assign the following roles:

• Story teller:

Every participant may have a turn.

• Listeners:

Encouraging, supporting the telling, asking questions to keep the flow of conversation going.

• Observers/Recorders:

Record emotions, what is said or expressed by the story teller on a flip chart or notepad.

4. Each group sets an expected time limit for a story. Five minutes is often enough, although sometimes people fill an hour. Let the story flow without hurry or interruption. Check with the story teller for any desired conditions concerning the recording of the story or specific ways to be encouraging.

5. Be specific when telling your story:

- "In March of 1988, I..."

- "Jack went to the San Antonio circus twice that winter.

Tell the story from your perspective or you can speak from the third person. Include conversations, gestures, props, or quotes from other people, anything that adds to elements of the story. When the story ends leave a moment of silence, so the story teller and others can reflect.

6. After Each Story:

Ask observers for major themes, points, and comments about the story. The observer records these on a flip chart. Extract the values implied in the story items. Highlight or prioritize the values. Review the interpretation and values with the story teller.

THEMES	VALUES
——————	——————
——————	——————
——————	——————
——————	——————
——————	——————
——————	——————
——————	——————

7. After All Stories Have Been Told:

Collect all value lists and identify common qualities and shared concerns. Review the problem statement to see what actions might be taken by the values indicated in the story. Example actions might be: work assignments, career steps,.and purchase equipment. Collect and compare value-action statements for their individual and group feasibility.

ASSIGNMENTS
———————————
———————————
———————————
———————————
———————————

VALUE

GROUP SIZE: *3 or more people. A facilitator will be important with groups of more than 12 people.*

TIME REQUIREMENTS: *Small groups of less than 5 people will take about 2 hours. A larger group will take half a day.*

SPACE FACILITIES: *A non-office atmosphere: a dining table, fireplace, or club room. Wall space to hang charts.*

REFERENCES:
Reason, P. (1988).
Keen, S. (1988).
Akin, G. (1990).

ALLOCATE

MOVING TO WHERE IT MATTERS

PURPOSE: *To clarify the participants' positions on an issue and make space in which to change opinions.*

OUTCOMES: *A vivid image of how each person sees their relationship to an issue. A new vocabulary used to talk about the resolution and new directions.*

COMMENTS: *The value of this tool is in the physical representation of images. It uncovers patterns and opinions that are useful in arriving at solutions. There are many varieties of this tool. We described two.*

SAMPLE USES:

• *Working an issue before it has been clearly formulated.*

• *Informal voting on a complex issue.*

"YOUR PLACE IN THE ORGANIZATION"

(Use this version for situations such as organizational design, power conflicts, and coordination efforts.)

1. **Place a 12 foot cardboard arrow in the center of a bare floor.** Tell the participants that the arrow represents the core process of their organization. Ask them individually and silently to associate parts of the arrow and the surrounding space with the particular activities in the organization. For example, note places where acquiring, converting, managing, and directing are done.

2. **Ask people to move to the place on or around the arrow that matches their responsibilities.** There may be competition for places. Work these out until everyone is settled. The participants may sit if they think they will be in that position for a long time. Progress around the room asking each person to define the arrow and their reason for choosing the space they occupy.

3. **Open conversation to argue around the definition of the arrow, the surrounding space, and places people have chosen.** Collect the major themes on a flip chart for everyone to view. If the core definition of the arrow and space changes have the participants move to the new space that represents their position. Again open the conversation to comments and reinterpretation.

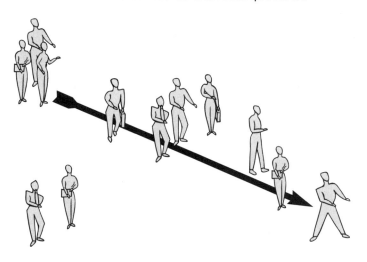

"HOMESTEADING"

(Use this version to define issues and identify individual's positions.)

1.   Define a large square on the floor—20 feet or more on each side. Inform the participants that the square represents the space of their options. Ask someone who has a clear statement of their position on the issue to state their position. Then, ask that person to move to a place in the square that represents that position. Ask a second person to describe their position and move to a place that best represents their position relative to the first person's position. Repeat this step, adding 2-4 more people who find their positions in reference to others. Anyone may change position to better define their opinion.

2.   Ask the remaining participants to move into the square, taking positions they feel best identifies their "stance" relevant to those of the original 4-6 positions. Each person should move close to those with whom they agree and appropriately distant from those with whom they disagree.

3.   When everyone has a place ask the people with the extreme positions to express their opinions and to indicate discomforts about the positions they have taken. As new opinions are expressed encourage people to move around to more suitable spots.

4.   When everyone has settled form a description of the "space of opinion." Count those clustered around popular spots. Label the dimensions that are implied by the positionings: conservative, liberal, humanistic, technocratic, etc. Identify opinion leaders and people who think from specific Realities: Unitary, Sensory, Social, and Mythic. Discuss the new ideas that arise from this presentation of opinions.

ALLOCATE

GROUP SIZE: *15 people and up. Ideal around 20-40 people.*

TIME REQUIREMENTS: *30 minutes to one hour.*

SPACE FACILITIES: *Most versions of this exercise require large spaces. A minimum of 20 square feet.*

PREPARATION: *Form the floor figures in advance.*

EQUIPMENT: *Cardboard, rope, or wide tape.*

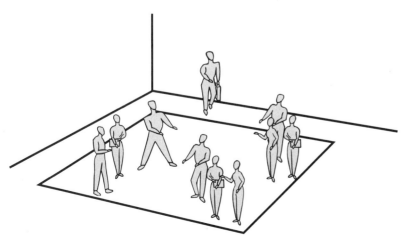

ALLOCATE

RESOURCE ALLOCATION

PURPOSE: *To assign or distribute resources participatively, applying an agreed upon value system.*

OUTCOMES: *A budget or allocation of resources and responsibilities.*

COMMENTS: *Allocation bases the distributions of goods and services on values. The following two allocating methods are used to help assign values and allocate goods, tasks, or obligations in two general situations.*

SAMPLE USES:

• *Sharing jobs within a team.*

• *Allocating a philanthropy's annual funds.*

ONE VALUE SYSTEM WITH MANY ALTERNATIVES

1. **List rules for valuating.** Have the participants list the values that are being used to make the allocation. For example, "Access to meaningful learning on the job." Form rules by which this value will be assigned to the resources. Such a rule would be, "No one will be denied access to training if a week's warning is given to supervisors prior to an event." Inevitably differences will show up among the group members. Prioritize the various rules in one list. Assign either a rank or a quality to indicate the strength with which each is valued. For example, "choice of training" is higher in rank than, "total training hours." You might vote on the importance of the quality or rule, summarize individually assigned priority lists, or assign some value between 1-100 to each rule to form a group weight for each alternative.

2. **Rank the rules for valuating.** List each of the tasks giving them assigned weights, ranking or point values. Assign employees to tasks to optimize overall competencies. (In the example below, tasks are ranked from 1-5. Assignment of employees to tasks are circled.)

EMPLOYEES

TASKS	KATE	JOHN	BILL	SUE	ANN	BOB
A	2	②	5	③	1	3
B	3	4	3	③	②	4
C	4	1	①	2	4	5
D	①	2	4	4	3	4
E	3	5	4	5	2	②

3. **Look for interactions among rules.** Notice where assignments interfere or support each other—you cannot do advanced training before completing basic, or considering how grants may be synergistic.

4. **Redesign the ranking.** Values are usually interdependent, so no matter how carefully the valuating process is done, the assignment will usually produce conflicts. In doing so, it produces a new awareness of interactions and opportunities.

MANY PEOPLE IN ONE COMMUNITY

This design is for a large team of 12-60 people, for a program that is expected to require extensive work.

1. Breakdown the work.

A focus group of under 12 people creates a breakdown of the total task working from known specifications and requirements. Draw on a large wall chart the overall relations and flow among the tasks. Have the group write each task on a card that will be assigned to a team member. Use a 9" x 5" card so the writing is big enough to read at a distance. Place these task cards at their appropriate place on the chart. This stage is extensive and might require many meetings over the span of weeks.

2. Determine tasks and abilities.

This is a day long team meeting. It must create a sense of community and good will. The process only works when there is an over-riding sense of fairness. The focus group presents a description of all the tasks. Each person lists their abilities and experience as they relate to the described tasks reflecting on the areas where they can potentially contribute to the effort. Have the participants "go shopping" for the task cards located on the overall chart, matching their abilities and experiences to the tasks. They add their names to the task cards to which they might contribute.

3. Form sub-groups for tasks.

Form sub-groups of people who want to work on sections of the total task. Participants within the sub-groups negotiate for assignments among themselves using repeated mini versions of Steps 1 and 2. They again write their names and abilities on the task cards to indicate their choices.

4. Work with a sense of community.

The focus group reviews the outcomes, noting omissions, over-assignments, and mismatches. Ideally they do this immediately and reform sub-groups to work the assignment issues until a balanced set of assignments is achieved.

5. Celebrate the achievement!

ALLOCATE

There are great variations among the processes described here, so no one set of specifications is proposed.

THE INVENTIVE MODE

The Inventive Mode is based on the material world—the rearranging of objects and ideas that are available but that have not been accessed. It depends on making an idea tangible, creating new concepts to make something, moving or destroying it, or transforming what we think is not a solution into something that is. The play is on the Fifth Board where new games are created. The Directional Methods of the Inventive Mode are Inducing and Realizing. Individuals with an entrepreneurial leadership style will tend to cycle between Realizing and Inducing as their preferred approach to planning, resolving conflicts, and affecting change.

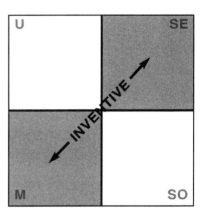

DIRECTIONAL METHODS

INDUCE

Inducing is the creation of an inclusive idea, symbol, or image that leads to the solution of a problem or provides understanding and meaning of an issue.

REALIZE

Realizing is putting an idea into practice. It details and materializes an idea, image, or symbol so that results can be achieved.

INDUCE

BRAINSTORMING

Brainstorming is a familiar and wonderful tool but there are many occasions when its power is neglected in favor of expediency. To get the most out of a *Brainstorming* session it is important to get into the proper mood.

PURPOSE: *To stimulate an uninhibited conference type, group approach to problem solving.*

OUTCOMES: *A large number of alternative ideas for later evaluation and development.*

SAMPLE USES:

• *Naming a project.*

• *Freeing yourself from habitual answers."*

• *Reframing a problem.*

• *Creating a new product.*

1. Warm up.

Do a 5 minute "humorous" brainstorming before doing the "real" brainstorming. For example, come up with answers for a question like: "What could you do with a 40 foot stalk of celery?"

2. Brainstorming ground rules.

Go over the following brainstorming ground rules before starting the session. Post them on a large flip chart for everyone to see.

**BRAINSTORMING
GROUND RULES**

LET IDEAS FLOW

SPEAK OUT

INSPIRE !!!

DON'T JUDGE

GO WITH THE FLOW

BE OUTRAGEOUS !!!

INDUCE

BRAINSTORMING IS...

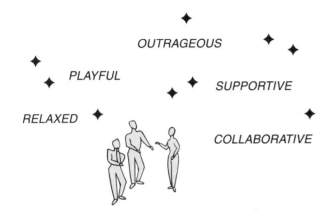

OUTRAGEOUS

PLAYFUL

SUPPORTIVE

RELAXED

COLLABORATIVE

GROUP SIZE: *3-11 people.*
5-9 people is optimal.

TIME REQUIREMENTS:
20 minutes minimum to half a
day.

SPACE FACILITIES: *Non-*
restricting space, protected
against outside interruptions.

EQUIPMENT: *Paper, "Post-*
its," pencils, flip charts, markers.

REFERENCES:
Morgan, G. (1993).

3. **The Process.**

   • Break into sub-groups of not more than 9 people. Large groups inhibit full participation and the ability to capitalize on everyone's ideas.

   • Agree on the group's task.

   • Refer to the brainstorming rules and go with the spirit.

4. **Record all ideas without editing.**

In a larger group one person can be assigned the job of listening and recording ideas on a flip chart. Another way to capture ideas is to have individuals write on "Post-its" and put them up as they are generated.

INDUCE

PURPOSE: *To make the familiar strange in the service of making the strange familiar. A method of finding highly creative responses to technical and social outcomes.*

COMMENTS: *The metaphoric methods set seemingly irrelevant, absurd, and contradictory framings to force us to work from new perspectives. Rather than avoiding constraints, as in the Brainstorming tool, the Metaphor tool locates a freshly constrained setting in which to apply analytic methods, poetic explorations, and bodily analogies to find solutions to the analogous problems.*

OUTCOMES: *Surprising and simple solutions, reframing of issues and new formulations that open new opportunities for exploration.*

SAMPLE USES:

• *Industrial design of processes and goods.*

• *Creation of new organizational forms.*

• *Reframing interpersonal conflicts.*

METAPHOR

1. Step away from the problem.

State the problem simply. For example, "A door that seals a space shuttle compartment won't open in zero gravity." Display this statement on a flip chart. Ask the whole group to find analogies by asking the question. "This is like...?" This question might get responses such as "A drunk trying to get keys out of his pocket." "When you are free, I am trapped." "A car engine at -40 degrees."

2. Build a metaphoric resolution.

Split into small groups of 2-7 people. Have the groups select an analogy, building a complete description of the solution in this analogous setting. Have them tell tales of how they solved the problem or describe new inventions or physical conditions. The description may include animals, science fiction, history, odd bits of technology, anything that contributes to the situation.

3. Revert to the problem environment.

Once the group has developed an attractive metaphoric tale of a solution, their task is to match the elements of the metaphor to that of the source problem. Participants create two lists: the structure and process in the metaphor, and elements of the problem situation that are analogous to the elements of the metaphor. Identify as many matches as possible. When there are many matches on critical aspects of the metaphorical solution it is likely to lead to a workable solution in the "real world." Occasionally, the metaphor setting is so close to the actual problem that a solution can be applied directly, resolving the problem. Even mismatches can provide the key to a solution.

4. Example: Shuttle door.

The table to the right considers the possible analogies between the stuck shuttle door and a drunk. Remember that unusual misfits frequently provoke insightful results!

THE DRUNK		SHUTTLE
"Tight"	=	Tight door
Stoned	=	Frozen
Free floating	=	Free floating
Crumpled over	??	No gravity!!
Can't get into pocket	=	Can't find sticking point
"Blind"	=	Can't get outside to see problem

4. Step into the Metaphor.

In this step the problem solver enters the environment playfully working with the Metaphor. Lay out the problem graphically in some detail. In the stuck door example, make a large cartoon drawing of the door and frame or the whole space shuttle. Working in small groups, one or more of the participants "becomes" some aspect of the problem. In the space shuttle example, your stomach might become the compartment. Talk from the experience of "stuckness" while floating in space. You will likely find unconventional solutions and processes, if you identify your body with the metaphor.

5. Step back into the problem.

As in step 3, set up a list of the qualities, actions, etc. in the metaphorical description. Then, systematically switch those back into the problem domain, noting the differences. In this stage it is useful to bring in new participants to test the fit as it goes along. Their concern with some of the absurdities can lead to even more insights.

6. Form a compressed conflict statement.

This step gets at another aspect of the metaphors, their non-logical, internally paradoxical nature. Again, creating such metaphors forces us to experience things strangely, thus enabling us to approach solutions from unconventional directions. The essence of this step is to form a self-contradictory description of the situation. A compressed conflict is a two-word provocation which causes one to look beyond the obvious.

For example, calcium was labeled as a "poisonous communicator" to help see its role in the body. The slightest excess of calcium threatens the life of a cell. It is a great messenger because a cell is very attentive to it and the messages it brings along.

Working with metaphorical descriptions, the small groups are encouraged to find such contradictory phrases. Some compressed conflicts appear as humorous oxymorons such as "military intelligence." The solutions come from the attempt to show how both aspects can be true.

INDUCE

GROUP SIZE: *Split any size group into subgroups of 7 or fewer people. Several subgroups working in the same space can stimulate ideas.*

TIME REQUIREMENTS: *This exercise profits from continuation over at least one night and more if the issue is important or complex. Individual sessions could profitably last for as little as 20 minutes to glance at a problem.*

SPACE FACILITIES: *Often the personal analogy work requires sequestered space large enough for animated play and simulation.*

PREPARATION: *Gather lots of knowledge about the issue, then take time to step away from the details.*

EQUIPMENT: *Unpredictable and extensive if the metaphors call for simulations.*

REFERENCES:
Gordon, W. J. J. (1965).
Johnson, M. (1987).
Grossman, S. R. (1988).

INDUCE

NEW GAME

This tool creates a new sequence of actions. When generating alternative ways of creating *New Games* you need skills with the following four techniques:

- *Brainstorming:* Defer judgement. Quantity breeds quality. The wilder the better. Seek association, combination, and improvement.

- Idea Recycling: Look for things that worked in the past that if reframed, combined, amplified, magnified, or rearranged would suggest new alternatives.

- Idea Searching: Global search in related and unrelated areas for possibilities using literature searches, benchmarking, and expert opinion. In searching unrelated areas for ideas, use analogies, and metaphors. Search analogous, parallel worlds using the *Metaphor* tool.

- Idea Appreciation: Search internally for pieces of solutions that exist but are in the early stages of development. Search for experiments in progress, glimmers of hope, weak signals of impending change, promising clues, and the mutterings of mavericks that if amplified and nurtured might produce ideas for alternatives.

PURPOSE: *To create a new approach, new ways of performing a function or an entirely new game that better meets the challenge you face.*

OUTCOMES: *Creation of a new game, approach, process, or product.*

SAMPLE USES:

- *Redesign a work process.*

- *Develop new products and services.*

- *Design new competitive strategies.*

- *Develop an entirely new game.*

- *Create alternative scenarios.*

1. **Describe the current approach** to the problem by listing the steps in the process, the elements of the function, or the aspects of the issue. Place the steps in the current game on header cards and mount them on a flip chart as shown below.

CURRENT APPROACH:

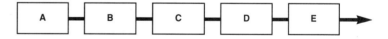

2. **Develop alternative ways** of accomplishing or thinking about each step, element, or aspect by:

- *Brainstorming* ways of accomplishing or thinking about each header card. Place the brainstormed ideas or cards under the appropriate heading.

- Consolidate and refine the idea cards so that each entry represents a distinct alternative way of accomplishing or thinking about the header card.

3. **Create a new combination** of the existing and alternative steps by interconnecting ideas in each column. Each string of alternatives is a possible *New Game*. Choose one or two of the most compelling and interesting *New Games* for further refinement. Construct a diagram following the general pattern of the following example.

4. **Example: Design of the *USA Today* Newspaper.**

    • Describe the current approach. The major aspects of current daily newspaper publishing are listed across the top of the page. The current approach is shown by path "A."

    • Develop alternatives under each aspect. List various choices for each aspect under that header card.

    • Create new combinations. The *New Game* of *USA Today* is shown by line "B." Other possible new designs would utilize different combinations of the alternative aspects.

ASPECTS OF NEWSPAPER PUBLISHING:

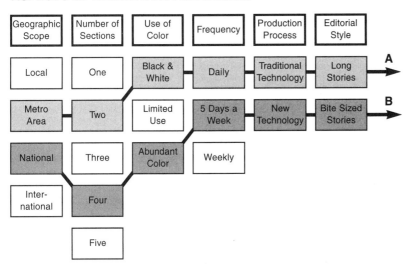

A = The old game of newspaper publishing as of the introduction of *USA Today* in 1982. Following the introduction, other newspapers copied many of its aspects.

B = The new game of newspaper publishing created by Gannett Publishing under the leadership of Al Neuharth.

A good way to warm-up is to have the group plot the old and new games of toy retailing exemplified by the emergence of "Toys R Us."

INDUCE

GROUP SIZE: *7 people is ideal. You need a mixture of those familiar with the process of function and those who can ask fresh questions and propose new alternatives.*

TIME REQUIREMENTS: *1-3 hours for a simple process. Two to three days in a retreat setting for a major effort at creating a new game.*

SPACE FACILITIES: *Wall space for mounting header cards on flip chart pages.*

PREPARATION: *Some of the involved people must be well grounded in the current process. Leader must know how to encourage creative thinking.*

EQUIPMENT: *Flip charts, header cards, or adhesive notes.*

DATA: *Background materials for triggering idea recycling, idea search, and idea appreciation. Description of the current function, process, or "game."*

REFERENCES: *Webber, J. (1991).*

INDUCE

PURPOSE: *To test and break the trap of role assignments by playfully violating these assumptions. To evoke new images of how an organization can be structured and how to place its boundaries.*

OUTCOMES: *Such play will find all manners of new assignments, many will be inappropriate, but a few may make remarkable differences in how an organization works.*

SAMPLE USES:

• *Create new markets.*

• *Reframe an organization.*

• *Explore alternative power relationships among groups in a community.*

ROLE ASSIGNMENTS

The assumptions we make about the roles we should play frequently block our ability to respond constructively to new issues. We assume the roles we take on and the corresponding functions to be necessary building blocks of our organization. By freeing ourselves from this assumption and repackaging the various tasks of the organization into a new structure, we can gain great awareness. *Role Assignments* is used when re-engineering or reallocation cannot achieve the needed change.

1. List.

List the major functions and stakeholders to an operation. For example, in a university: sources of money, suppliers, students, administration, trustees, and faculty.

2. Reassign roles.

• Reassign the functions and the roles, making random pairings. Create images of what it would be like if these assignments were made. For example, assign the role of faculty to the students and that of maintenance to the trustees. Explore the implications of such role assignments, no matter how absurd they appear on the surface.

• Try multiple assignments, e.g., view students as workers and product, or administrators as learners and consumers.

• Invent new roles and deny conventional ones. For example, see what would change if customers were reinvented as "co-producers" who create rather than consume values.

3. Construct metaphors.

Construct roles from a metaphorical image. In place of the organizational type roles with which you are working try the roles in:

- A zoo
- An orchestra
- The Catholic Church

When you have found assignments that are insight producing, begin to build a scenario of the organization with the role changes, adding whatever is provocative.

4. Brainstorm.

Proceed as in the *Brainstorming* tool located on page 176. Play with assignments without judgment to encourage the group to make and explore outrageous assignments.

5. Reflect.

Ideally, you should stop when the *Brainstorming* winds down. Record what you did, then "sleep" on the ideas over night, over a weekend, or at most over a week.

Have the same people reassemble and review and evaluate. The outcomes may be surprising "answers" to the problem.

3. Example: Role switching to induce new ideas.

Consider reversing the roles of Joe, the student, and his teacher Mrs. Peabody. Joe assumes the role of the "teacher," and Mrs. Peabody the "student."

- As a "teacher" Joe would use his power to extract information from Mrs. Peabody the "student."

- Mrs. Peabody as a "student" is responsible for giving good information, but is no longer responsible for the structure and control of the eduction.

 INDUCE

GROUP SIZE: *3-12 people. Divide larger groups into 5-7 people.*

TIME REQUIREMENTS: *2 hours in the initial session. The follow-up could be the beginning of a major redesign effort.*

EQUIPMENT: *Flip charts.*

REFERENCES: *Normann, R. & Ramirez, R. (1994).*

REALIZE

PURPOSE: *To create plans in a way that greatly increases the potential for achieving them.*

OUTCOMES: *A story that frees a group to take actions toward a desired future.*

COMMENTS: *The name Future Perfect is from the verb tense for what in the future will have happened.*

SAMPLE USES:

• *Project planning to initiate a defined activity in an organization or community.*

• *A brainstorming session about processes and feasibility.*

• *An initiatory device to get a blocked activity moving.*

FUTURE PERFECT

This is story telling about what you will have done in the future to solve a problem. You fantasize what steps lead you to a solution, then make the steps actually happen as though this path to a solution is your "fate." The story is about what you did do in the future to end up with some, often surprising, solution. The ideal future is not predetermined; it emerges from the story of how you got to it.

1. **Prepare the participants.**

   • The facilitator (leader or outsider) describes the mechanism for creating a "certain future" that has occurred because of our tales of what *did happen.*

   • The individuals recall an actual event in which each by their own initiative made something happen and thus feel personally potent. Share recollections with others and discuss feelings of potency experienced in creating the world as they wished it.

Future Perfect requires a climate of belief in one's personal potential.

2. **Set the event.**

Describe a specific event at a date far enough in the future for the participants to believe it plausible that the described outcome could be achieved. It could be months or years away.

   • The event is or follows a celebration of achievement. It could be an award ceremony, a return home after a victory, or a report to the Board at which the participants share their memories of the achieved goal.

   • Enhance the setting with various theatrical devices, such as changes of seating, lighting, false calendars or clocks. Key all effects to the group to "create the future" in fantasy and fact.

3. **Begin the tale.**

Someone, usually the initiator, starts the tale by "remembering" the event that started the path to success. It could be the very event in which this tale is being told or some event that *did* happen the next day. The event is told explicitly as it happened in the past, with names, pieces of conversation, etc., even though it takes place at a future date.

4. Continue the tale.

When the initiator has finished, a second person "recalls" a subsequent event, building on the earlier one, showing what difficulties and successes emerged. As participants feel ready, they "recall" other memories, gradually moving toward the "future present." Each person tells of just one event at a time, building on the prior one, allowing each person to recall a piece of the group's history.

Record each event on a flip chart or wall board. Using a graphic artist to vividly portray the images greatly strengthens the feeling that these events "were" real.

The facilitator may take a role such as a newspaper reporter in order to give direction and pace to the telling process.

5. Some style pointers.

- The exercise loses effectiveness if a participant "recalls" the arrival of gifts from "heaven, the Lone Ranger, or the Ford Foundation." This leads to a passive sense that one cannot make things happen.

- Each story is accepted as a true memory of what happened. Each new memory adds to the story events that add new direction without denying what another already remembered.

6. Work with the memories.

If the tale was powerfully told the earliest remembered event becomes tomorrow's agenda. It just happens! More commonly, the group reviews the events from beginning to end, articulates the purpose for each event, noting who was present and the outcome. Events are then analyzed and resources identified. People and resources are assigned to the initial recalled event and the event is scheduled.

7. On-going remembering.

The tale is open ended. You can add in events, start subplots, and continue from where the story left off. Reflect on the implications to clarify the direction you should take. It's not a vision, it's happening. This approach differs significantly from the *Visioning* tool in that it does not require a specific vision of the future. It presents a connected history of the future. And, it begins with "past events" immediately following the occasion when the planning is done. The description is of what we actively chose to do, not of what was done to us.

REALIZE

GROUP SIZE: *3-12 people. Process needs an observer to be visioning while one talks and others listen. Groups larger than 12 have little opportunity for involvement. At least one participant should be of a dominantly Mythic Reality.*

TIME REQUIREMENTS: *A small group typically requires 2-3 hours for the tale and analysis.*

PREPARATION: *Obtaining a graphic artist to record the events greatly enhances the power of the process.*

EQUIPMENT: *Flip charts or poster walls.*

REFERENCES:
Ziegler, W. (1982).

REALIZE

LOTUS BLOSSOM

This is a tool for articulating ideas. It is more formal than *Mind Mapping* (page 192) and easier for people who prefer formula oriented tools versus creative problem solving tools. Results are often innovative and clear, and the work is enjoyable.

PURPOSE: *To develop the specifics of an idea in a highly visible way.*

OUTCOMES: *A Lotus Blossom diagram that elaborates and portrays the specifics of an idea or image.*

SAMPLE USES:

• *Developing needed specifics on an idea or image.*

1. Construct.

Construct a *Lotus Blossom* chart as shown below.

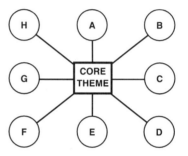

2. Identify core theme.

Place the idea, image, or core theme in the box at the center of the diagram.

3. Brainstorm.

Brainstorm the major attributes, features, or characteristics of the idea. Place these major sub-points labeled "A" through "H" in the circles around the central box.

4. Identify the major sub-points.

Place the major sub-points in the center of their appropriate boxes and brainstorm the attributes, features, or characteristics or each, as shown in the diagram below.

REALIZE

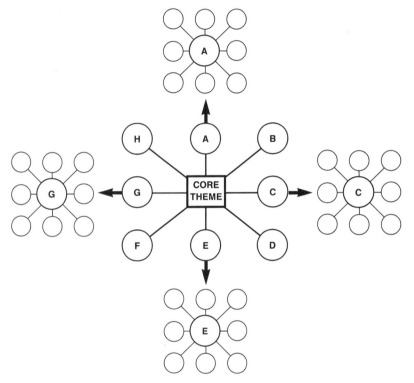

GROUP SIZE: *5-9 people.*

TIME REQUIREMENTS: *2-4 hours.*

SPACE FACILITIES: *A class or conference room.*

PREPARATION: *The initial created blank Lotus Blossom chart for each group.*

EQUIPMENT: *Flip charts, markers, and tape.*

REFERENCES: *Tatsuno, S. M. (1990).*

5. Extend the diagram.

Continue extending the diagram as required.

6. The finished diagram.

The finished *Lotus Blossom* diagram provides the full development of the idea.

The *Lotus Blossom* diagram is shown in matrix form in Tatsuno's book. By numbering each cell in the matrix, a concise action plan can be included next to the diagram.

THE EMERGENT MODE

The Emergent Mode is based on facilitating social interaction, creating or co-creating ideas or symbols and revaluing ideas. It depends on creating and gaining acceptance for an idea or symbol to create new meaning, make possible alternative actions and outcomes, and to transcend existing conflicts and limitations. The play is on the Sixth Board, where existing structures are transcended and meanings created, shaping opportunities for change. Change creates the values, purpose, strategies, and rules of the organization. The Directional Methods of the Emergent Mode are Evoking and Facilitating. Individuals with an Emergent leadership style will tend to cycle between Evoking and Facilitating as their preferred approach to planning, resolving conflict, and affecting change.

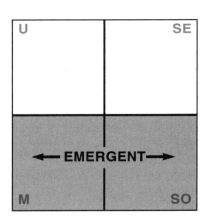

DIRECTIONAL METHODS

EVOKE

With the Evoking Mode, a group co-creates ideas and images that symbolize their values. The basic question is "Given what matters to us, what do we wish to create?" The values are assumed.

TOOL	PAGE
Core of Intent	190
Mind Mapping	192
Search Conference	194

FACILITATE

Facilitating has to do with gaining commitment to an idea, image or program by affecting the motivations, attitudes, and values of those involved. The power of an idea is its ability to change values and attract commitment.

TOOL	PAGE
Co-Generation	196
Innovation Process	198

EVOKE

PURPOSE: *To find a statement of the core intent for a person or organization.*

OUTCOMES: *One or more two-word phrases that characterize the intent of the individual or group involved.*

SAMPLE USES:

• *Identify intent and sharpen the statement of purpose of an organization.*

• *Problem clarification and problem finding.*

• *Create logos and themes.*

• *Deepen and broaden the scope of opportunities, as in Breakthrough Thinking.*

CORE OF INTENT

This is the ultimate tool for identifying intent. It forms the *Core of Intent* from a simply formed statement: a verb and a noun. That is, an *"-ing" doing word* such as "making" and an *outcome* word such as "toys" or "happiness." Examples would be: "satisfying work," "becoming me," and "generating meaning." In addition, the *"-ing"* words can also be adjectives—"becoming" is a quality of a person as well as an action.

1. **Preparation.**

   • Ideas come rapidly once the group starts working so establish clear structure and rules. Assign two people to write phrases on flip charts or wall board with markers. Illustrate the basic form and give some examples of the two-word phrases.

   • All phrases consist of exactly two words, the first ending in "ing," and the second being a noun or adjective. Never add articles ("the, a, an,...") or modifiers ("some, few, most,...").

   • State the desired outcomes, usually saying something like "Select pairs of words that capture the major thrust of the organization." Use the rules of *Brainstorming* let ideas flow freely, no self-censoring, no ridicule, and no negating an idea.

2. **The process (a simple version).**

The participants dump ideas as rapidly as they can, forming two separate lists: *"-ing"* words describing the doing and nouns or adjectives that describe the object of the intent. The word are recorded in separate lists so long as the dump continues. A typical group will produce 20-50 words per list before slowing. When slowing occurs begin the next step of cleaning up the lists by scratching duplicate words.

Have participants look for pairs of words, one from each list, that most sharply characterize their intent. Rewrite these pairs of words on a new sheet of paper. Forming pairs often evokes new words. Add these to the lists. Form new pairs until the group has run out of ideas or they converge on pairs that seem just right.

3. **An alternative process.**

Record the pairs of dumped words onto a single list. Immediately coming up with pairs evokes more images and produces more unusual ideas than listing words separately, although it takes more creativity to get this variation rolling. Working with pairs leads to playing with words, metaphors, and double meanings that deepen the exploration.

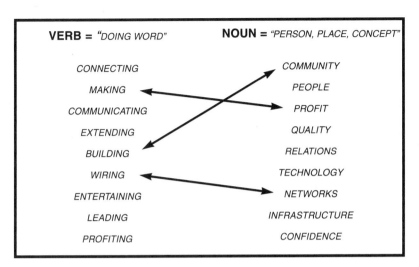

> **VERB** = *"DOING WORD"*   **NOUN** = *"PERSON, PLACE, CONCEPT"*
>
> CONNECTING   COMMUNITY
>
> MAKING   PEOPLE
>
> COMMUNICATING   PROFIT
>
> EXTENDING   QUALITY
>
> BUILDING   RELATIONS
>
> WIRING   TECHNOLOGY
>
> ENTERTAINING   NETWORKS
>
> LEADING   INFRASTRUCTURE
>
> PROFITING   CONFIDENCE

EVOKE

GROUP SIZE: *Any size.*

TIME REQUIREMENTS: *A few minutes up to 2 hours for a multistage effort.*

PREPARATION: *Many groups can benefit by playing word games before starting this work.*

EQUIPMENT: *Two flip charts or a long wall chart.*

REFERENCES:
Nadler, G. & Hibino, S. (1990).

4. Capture the *Core of Intent*.

- The exercise is completed by selecting 1-4 pairs that capture the *Core of Intent*. This can be done by consensus, ranking, or voting. The pairs may stand by themselves or be integrated into a phrase that captures the same idea and feeling.

- A group of pairs can be organized graphically to create a logo. Or they may be ordered in a ladder of increasing scope. One company following a progression from "Building Roads" to "Relating People" and finally to "Enabling Resources."

5. Example: The telephone company:

In the late 1970's Bell and other telephone companies were struggling to find their role in the new communications industries. In exercises with two different companies the dominant image was captured in the pair of words "extending me." This followed the century old dogma of American telephone companies that the system was designed for serving individuals. In a third company, a rich word plan developed following a slip of the tongue in which one executive suggested :"infra-ing structure" This term led to the more manageable "Infrastructuring America," and "Networking America." Adopting this intent was an element in refocusing that company's efforts to see the telephone system as a fundamental highway system for communication in the coming decades.

EVOKE

PURPOSE: *To evoke ideas and new words that allow an individual or group to reframe or reformulate a problem.*

OUTCOMES: *One or more words and related organization of ideas that lead to the solution of a problem or eliminate the source of conflict.*

SAMPLE USES:

• *Problem formulation.*

• *Reorganize ideas that are in conflict.*

• *Repackage services and features of a product.*

• *Name newly formed concepts.*

• *Unblock thinking.*

• *Self-organize material one is learning from a text (school work).*

MIND MAPPING

Mind mapping promotes free association of ideas and reveals new meanings for familiar concepts. It provides paths around our normal self-censoring and supports joint intuitive right brain work in a group.

1. **Create the mind map.**

   • Start with an over-sized blank sheet of paper. Select a single word or phrase that represents the motivating focus. Print it in large capital letters in the middle of the paper.

   • Settle back and let your mind free associate about the focal word. Let words pop out of your mind. Print them in capital letters anywhere on the paper. Underline or connect them to the focus if it feels appropriate. Underlining, printing, and connecting all help bring out new gestalts from the right brain. Continue printing and connecting words as they tumble into your consciousness. Make additional connections where you sense them.

   • Keep your printing large and legible. Add graphics and color if you wish. Let the words continue to tumble unabated. When the ideas stop, sit back and scan your image, waiting for new words to emerge. The tumbling may start again at any time. When the page is full, you feel pressed for time, or you are blocked, move to the next step.

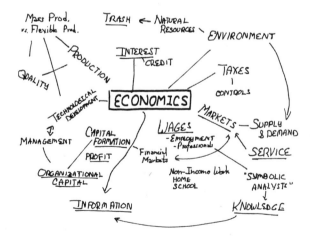

2. Redraw.

- Gently scan your work with curiosity for what you have done. Look for clusters that form elements of the main focus or an alternative focus. You might have half a dozen. Wipe over each of these words with a highlighter pen of a different color. Color code every word by its association with one of the highlighted words. You will see new clusters emerging.

- Print the focal word on a new sheet and organize highlighted terms on the map where you sense they should go. Move all the terms that are color coded to the new sheet, connecting them as you see fit. Create new connections and more terms, working until you run out of ideas or time. If you see a new organization of ideas emerging *redraw a second time*. Merge your map with others who have been working on the task.

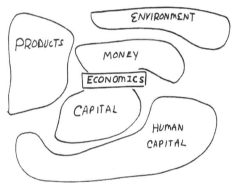

3. The final map.

The final mapping includes new formulations of ideas that had not been articulated by those involved. New symbols, new terms, new relations give openings for new research, observations, and policies. In this example, the old trio of capital, labor, and land are replaced with an economics about information, human values, and the environment.

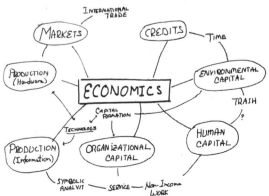

EVOKE

GROUP SIZE: *1-5 people. The products of many groups can be merged into one map.*

TIME REQUIREMENTS: *A single map can be done in a half hour. A full mapping by a large group might be done over several days.*

PREPARATION: *Plan to have deeply experienced people intermixed with inexperienced people who usually work through intuition.*

EQUIPMENT: *Large paper sheets, 14" x 17" for individuals, and 4' x 4' for a group.*

REFERENCES: *Buzan, T. (1983).*

EVOKE

PURPOSE: *To establish the set of values held by various stakeholders, bundling them together to guide the search for practical resolutions.*

OUTCOMES: *An organized list of stakeholder priorities, concerns, and values that must be respected in the creation of a solution. Often the conference produces a core metaphor that guides the subsequent path of resolution.*

SAMPLE USES:

• *The technique was developed for working with regional issues that may effect a community, metropolitan district, or even a small nation.*

• *It can be used in major international conflicts, gang warfare, urban renewal and occasionally with internal corporate issues.*

• *A conference may be called to found a new institution such as a health center, museum, or school.*

SEARCH CONFERENCE

A *Search Conference* is usually called when the issue involves a whole community where no single institution responsible for resolution. It is particularly useful when the stakeholders do not share or know each other's values. In their participation the stakeholders form a common image of the desired outcome.

This tool involves a lot of people and time. It is begins Evaluatively but comes to fruition in the Evocative mode. It is important that participants attend all conference related meetings. Attending the conference enhances the power of the participants. Leaving out any interest group can open conflicts that will derail every proposed solution. As a Renaissance tool, it is almost certain to disturb establishment policies and leadership.

1. Plan the conference.

Form a small planning group including an outside facilitator and local organizers. This planning group formulates a statement of the issue and invites people in the stakeholder groups who should attend the conference. The group sets schedules and meeting sites and creates a workable budget. A pre-meeting dinner can be used to raise money, sharpen the issue focus, and build enthusiasm.

2. Hold the conference.

Open with explanations of the process and the generally expected outcomes. Avoid advocacy for any positions. Describe the broad setting of the issue to assure all stakeholders see the entire domain of the issue. Establish a democratic climate to assure everyone feels safe in expressing their opinions.

3. Determine issue values.

Each group works to uncover their values around the issue. The *Pseudo-Quote* and *Metaphor* tools may help extract priorities, values, and constraints.

4. Explore the value implications.

Consider the ability of the community to respond to their values and needs.

5. Create scenarios for desired futures.

Break out of assumed present constraints. Create scenarios for desired futures using the *Brainstorming* or *Future Perfect* tools.

6. Evoke a metaphor.

The power of a *Search Conference* is greatest when it evokes a vibrant metaphor or story of how the community will work the issue.

7. Envision major tasks.

Identify the steps needed to develop plans and action for designing the future.

8. Form a task group and commit to action.

The conference must conclude with agreements on a schedule of follow-up meetings and responsibilities to assure action.

9. Example: A community *Search Conference*.

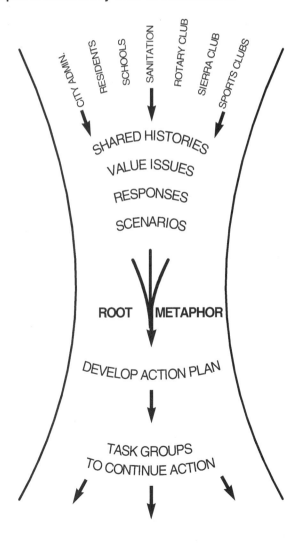

 EVOKE

GROUP SIZE: *12-24 people can be organized as a single group. More than 25 participants calls for a complex design with a staff of facilitators.*

TIME REQUIREMENTS: *A small conference can accomplish its mission in 2-3 days. Larger groups might need 4-5 days, or possibly two 3-day events separated by a couple weeks.*

SPACE REQUIREMENTS: *A residential setting is optimal, remote from the participants' residences and businesses. A large community room and break-out rooms for sub-groups.*

PREPARATION: *Research the history of the issue, exploring possible outcome scenarios and anticipating problems.*

EQUIPMENT: *Flip charts for recording meetings, facilities for copying sub-group work and changing agenda.*

REFERENCES:
Emery & Parser (1996).
Morely, D. (1987).
Weisbord, M. (1992).

FACILITATE

PURPOSE: *To co-generate a solution based on a "seed" idea provided by a leader.*

OUTCOMES: *A co-generated solution for which the group takes ownership.*

SAMPLE USES:

• *Gaining adoption for an idea proposed by any group member.*

CO-GENERATION

A dominantly Mythic person would not admit to using a tool to get a group to co-create an idea. For the Mythic the idea exists the moment they have it. So co-creation is procreation. The Mythic *gives* the idea to others to be worked generatively into a full blown design or solution. What seems to an outsider to be manipulative and inauthentic is for the Mythic person an act of commitment and personal responsibility. In using a tool under the direction of a Mythic leader, the participants may know both that they are being manipulated and that they can enjoy the empowerment from co-generation.

1. **Bring the idea to fruition.**

   • The premise of this tool is that you, the initiator, have both an image of the problem and an idea for a solution. Your task is to bring the idea to fruition. However, a population that is dominantly Social will demand participation in forming the solution.

   • The double dilemma is that you want both your idea and constructive acceptance. The participants want both a good idea and the sense that they have participated in its construction and adoption.

2. **Explore the problem.**

   • You and perhaps another change agent review the problem. You search for conditions that make an imagined solution weak or to find an alternative that is indistinguishably good or bad.

   • When exploring and testing your idea you become so sure of it that it moves from being your idea to being one that will serve the participants' needs. The idea need not be defended because its essence will naturally be a part of any solution. In doing so, you separate the idea and your ego.

2. Working the Solution.

- You do not present the original problem to your group. Rather you give them your incomplete solution as the problem. So you say, "I have a solution to a problem that I think is not yet workable. It needs your help."
- Your idea becomes the organizing difficulty in the solution effort. The group's task is to find how to strengthen, broaden, or replace it. Ultimately they must find a solution that you collectively know is a workable solution on which to base the issue.
- You as the idea provider must join the conversation without defending your idea. As a Mythic, you know your idea is a natural solution. It will not fail to solve the base issue if it gains full acceptance and support of the participants.

3. *Co-Generation*, organizing the task.

- Once you have prepared the group to work the reformulated problem, you step out of the initiator role and let the group self-organize.
- You may continue to reinforce your interpretation of the problem statement and play the role of the boundary manager to work the logistics.
- When accomplishing the task the participants now identify what is important to them in generating a satisfactory form of your idea. They select whatever tools are appropriate for further development and implementation of the idea, broadening and finalizing the solution.

4. Reflect.

This process as described may lead to the adoption of an idea. A second and important outcome is the resulting empowerment of the participants. Group members are assured by achieving a solution without the direction from you, the leader.

Have the group discuss the process that led them from the adoption of the idea to a solution. That is, the realization that they can reformulate any problem and take charge. They learn that task leadership is only one of the required roles for getting a task done.

 FACILITATE

All the detailed specifications will come from the tools you chose to work the reformulated problem.

PREPARATION: *This kind of needs a level of patience and insight many people find difficult to attain.*

FACILITATE

PURPOSE: *To get others interested in and willing to adapt and support the development of innovative ideas.*

OUTCOMES: *Others understand, believe in, and support the value of your innovative ideas.*

SAMPLE USES:

• *New product.*

• *New processes.*

• *New services.*

INNOVATION PROCESS

When using this tool be prepared for a long term commitment. Be persistent, believe in your dreams, and be willing to take a leap of faith.

1.   Write a clear concise idea statement.

Develop an explanation of the idea which anyone could understand. Try it out on a friend or student, anyone unfamiliar with the situation.

2.   Gather information.

Talk to people who have been successful innovators at your site. Ask them about improving your idea and how to respond to the criticisms you anticipate. Do your homework about costs, locate resources to develop the idea, identify other similar ideas that are already in use. Determine who the decision makers are who must support your idea.

3.   Develop goals and a plan.

Decide what your goals are with respect to your idea, the people they will involve and what you need from the organization to attain your goals. Establish a plan, such as the following steps, before doing any promotion of the idea.

4.   Be prepared to discuss the good, the bad, and the ugly.

List the advantages and disadvantages of your idea from the perspective of:

  • Yourself
  • Your immediate supervisor
  • Management
  • Your site
  • The corporation

Be able to state clearly the advantages from each of these perspectives. Decide how you will respond to the disadvantages from each perspective. Prepare yourself to listen to and respond appropriately to feedback of the idea.

Analyze the aspects of the process which you do and do not control. Think about what adjustments and compromises you are willing to make. Be aware of the ways in which feedback may be positive and helpful.

5. Develop a supportive team.

Identify a group of people who can provide both personal and organizational support for you and your idea. Identify which people will go to bat for you.

6. Prepare to present the idea.

Decide who will present the idea. Determine what should be presented, and pick the time and setting.

7. Present the idea.

Use good communication and negotiation techniques, maintaining a positive problem-solving posture. Present the idea briefly and clearly. Listen carefully and be positive and flexible. Involve the decision maker in problem solving and generating options for implementation.

8. Negotiate for implementation, work together.

- Work toward agreement, making changes as necessary. Summarize any objections that needs to be addressed. Ask about the probability of implementation if the objections can be addressed.

- State your summary of the discussion and the next steps and check the accuracy. Prepare a follow-up document which summarizes the discussion and the next steps.

9. Evaluate and repeat as necessary.

Take stock of where you are. Decide what to do next: get input, keep going, or step back and begin over.

10. Maintain a non-threatening approach.

If you get to a place in this process that requires skills that you do not have, either formulate and utilize team members, or get outside help from different specialists.

 FACILITATE

GROUP SIZE: *Individuals or groups.*

TIME REQUIREMENTS: *Several months to several years.*

SPACE FACILITIES: *Your everyday work environment, conference room or auditorium for final presentation.*

PREPARATION: *You just need an idea and an understanding of the stages of innovation.*

REFERENCES:
Grossman, S. R. (1988).
Musashi, M. (1982).

REFERENCES

Ackoff, Russell L (1978). *The Art of Problem Solving.* New York: John Wiley.

Ackoff, Russell L. (1981). *Creating the Corporate Future.* New York: John Wiley.

Adams, James L. (1986). *Conceptual Blockbusting.* Reading, MA: Addison-Wesley.

Akin, Gib (1990). Jazz Bands and Missionaries: OD Through Stories and Metaphor. *Journal of Managment Psychology* 5(4):12-18.

Argyris, Chris (1982). *Reasoning, Learning & Action.* San Francisco: Jossey-Bass.

Bandler, Richard (1985). *Using Your Brain— For a Change.* Moab, UT: Real People Press.

Beckhard, Richard, & Pritcher, William (1992). *Changing the Essence: the Art of Creating and Leading Fundamental Changes in Organizations.* San Francisco: Jossey-Bass.

Block, Peter (1986). *Empowered Manager: Positive Political Skills at Work.* San Francisco: Jossey-Bass.

Blohm, H. & Steinbuch, K. (1973). Technology Forecasting in Practice. London: Saxon House.

Bransford, John & Stein, Barry (1984). *The Ideal Problem Solver.* New York: W. H. Freeman Books.

Brassard, M. (1989). *The Memory Jogger Plus.* Methuen, MA: Goal.

Brookfield, Steven D. (1980). *Developing Critical Thinkers.* San Francisco: Jossey-Bass.

Brown, L. David (1983). *Managing Conflict at Organizational Interfaces.* Reading, MA: Addison Wesley.

Burke, James (1978). *Connections.* Boston: Little, Brown & Co.

Buzan, Tony (1983). *The Brain User's Guide.* New York: Dutton Paperback.

Buzan, Tony (1983). *Use Both Sides of Your Brain.* New York: Dutton Paperback.

Buzan, Tony (1984). *Make the Most of Your Mind.* Lidon Press/Simon & Schuster.

Checkland, Peter (1981). *Systems Thinking, Systems Practice.* Chichester, UK: John Wiley & Sons.

Cohen, A. R. & Bradford, D. L. (1990). *Influence Without Authority.* New York: John Wiley & Sons.

Cooperrider, D. L. & Srivastva, S. (1990). *Appreciative Management & Leadership.* San Francisco: Jossey-Bass.

Cowen, Thomas D. (1984). *How to Tap Into Your Own Creative Genius.* New York: Simon & Schuster.

de Bono, Edward (1973). *Lateral Thinking: Creativity Step by Step.* New York: Harper & Row.

de Bono, Edward (1978). *Opportunities: A Handbook of Business Opportunity Search.* Hammondsworth, Middlesex, England: Penguin Books.

de Bono, Edward (1993). *Serious Creativity: Using the Power of Lateral Thinking to Create New Ideas.* Harper Business.

Deal, Terrence E. & Kennedy, Allen K. (1982). *Corporate Cultures.* Reading, MA: Addison Wesley.

Deming, W. Edwards (1986). *Out of the Crisis.* Cambridge, MA: MIT, Center for Advanced Engineering Study.

Dewar, Donald (1991). *Employee Involvement Team Leader Manual & Instruction Guide.* Red Bluff, CA: QCI International.

Dilts, Cf. Robert (1983). *Applications of Neuro-Linguistic Programming.* Meta Publications

Dreyfus, Hubert & Dreyfus, Stuart (1986). *Mind Over Machine.* New York: Free Press.

Edwards, Betty (1986). *Drawing on the Artist Within.* New York: Simon & Schuster.

Edwards, Betty (1979). *Drawing on the Right Side of the Brain.* Los Angeles: Tarcher, J. P., distributed by St. Martin's Press, New York.

Emery, Merrilyn & Parser, Ron (1996). *The Search Conference.* San Francisco: Jossey-Bass.

Fanning, Robert (1988). *Visualization for Change.* Oakland, CA: New Harbinger Publications.

Gemmill, G. & Costello (1990). Group Mirroring. *Consultation* 9(4).

Gordon, W. J. J. (1961). *Synetics.* New York: Harper.

Gordon, W. J. J. (1973). *The Metaphorical Way of Learning and Knowing.* Porpoise Books.

Grossman, S. R., et. al. (1988). *Innovations, Inc. Unlocking Creativity in the Workplace.* Plano, TX: Wordward Publishing, Inc.

Hammer, Michael & Champy, James (1993). *Re-engineering the Corporation.* New York: Harper Business.

Hampden-Turner, Charles (1981). *Maps of the Mind.* New York: MacMillan.

Hampden-Turner, Charles (1990). *Charting the Corporate Mind: Graphic Solutions.* New York: Free Press.

Hanks, Kurt & Belliston, Larry (1980). *Rapid Viz: A New Method for the Rapid Visualization of Ideas.* Los Altos, CA: William Kaufman Books, Inc.

Hofstadter, Douglass R. (1982). *The Mind's I.* New York: Bantam.

Imai, Masaaki (1986). Kaizen, *The Key to Japan's Competitive Success.* New York: Random House

Ishikawa, Kaoru (1985). *What is Total Quality Control?: The Japanese Way.* Englewood Cliffs, NJ: Prentice-Hall.

Johnson, Leo (1991). *Understanding & Managing Conflict.* Unpublished.

Johnson, Mark (1987). *The Body in the Mind.* Chicago: University of Chicago Press.

Keen, Sam (1988). Stories We Live By. *Psychology Today.* December.

Kepner, Charles H. & Tregoe, Benjamin B. (1981). *The New Rational Manager.* Princeton: Princeton Research Press.

Kolb, David A. (1984). *Experiential Learning.* Englewood Cliffs, NJ: Prentice-Hall.

Laborde, Genie Z. (1983). *Influencing with Integrity.* Palo Alto, CA: Science & Behavior Books: Syntony Publishing Company.

Lewin, Kurt (1951). *Field Theory in Social Science.* New York: Harper & Row.

Loye, David (1984). *The Sphinx and the Rainbow.* New York: Bantam Books.

Mason, Richard & Mitroff Ian (1981). *Challenging Strategic Planning Assumptions.* New York: Wiley.

May, Rollo (1975). *The Courage to Create.* New York: Bantam Books.

McWhinney, Will (1993). *Myths & Stories in Organizational Change.* Venice, CA: Enthusion, Inc.

McWhinney, Will (1992). *Paths of Change.* Newbury Park, CA: Sage Publications.

Michalko, Michael (1991). *Thinkertoys: A Handbook of Business Creativity for the 90's.* Berkeley, CA: Ten Speed Press.

Misuno, S. (1988). *Management of Quality Improvement: The 7 New QC Tools.* Cambridge, MA: Productivity Press.

Morgan, Gareth (1993). *Imaginization.* Newbury Park, CA: Sage Publications.

Morley, David (1987). *An Introduction to Search Conferences.* Toronto: York University.

Musashi, Miyamoto (1982). *The Book of Five Rings.* New York: Bantam Books.

Nadler, G. & Hibino, S. (1990). *Breakthrough Thinking.* Rocklin, CA: Prima Publishing.

Normann, Richard & Ramírez, Raphel (1994). *Designing Interactive Strategies.* New York: John Wiley & Sons.

Nutt, P. C. & Backoff, W. (1993). Strategic Issues as Tensions. *Journal Management Inquiry* 2(1).

Ostrander, Sheila & Schhroeder, Lynn (1979). *Superlearning.* Delta Books.

Owen, Harrison (1987). *Spirit: Transformation and Development in Organizations.* Potomac, MD: Abbot Publishing.

Pahl, G. & Beitz, W. (1984). *Engineering Design.* Translated & Edited by K. M. Wallace. London: The Design Council.

Parker, Marjorie (1990). *Creating Shared Vision.* Clarendon Hills, IL: Dialog International Ltd.

Ray, Michael & Meyers, R. (1986). *Creativity in Business.* Garden City, NY: Doubleday & Co., Inc.

Reason, Peter, Ed. (1988). *"Storytelling as Inquiry"* in *Human Inquiry in Action.* Newbury Park, CA: Sage Publications.

Rhodes, Jerry (1991). *Conceptual Toolmaking.* Cambridge, MA: Basil Blackwell Publishers.

Rowe, A. J., et. al. (1989). *Strategic Management: A Methodological Approach.* Reading, MA: Addison Wesley.

Rubinstein, Moshe & Pfeffer, Kenneth (1980). *Concepts in Problem Solving.* Englewood Cliffs, NJ: Prentice-Hall.

Schein, Edgar (1985). *Organizational Culture and Leadership.* San Francisco, CA: Jossey-Bass.

Scholtes, Peter R. (1988). *The Team Handbook.* Madison, WI: Joiner Associates, Inc.

Senge, Peter (1990). *The Fifth Discipline.* NY: Doubleday.

Senge, Peter; Kleiner, Art; Roberts, Charlotte; Ross, Rick & Smith, Byron (1994). *The Fifth Discipline Fieldbook.* New York: Currency/Doubleday.

Tassoul, Marc (1992) "Selective Confrontation" in *Creativity and Innovation: Quality Breakthroughs.* Ed. by Tudor Richards, Susan Moger, Patrick Colemont and Marc Tassoul. Delft, The Netherlands: Innovation Consulting Group.

Tatsuno, Sheridan M. (1990). *Created in Japan.* New York: Harper & Row.

Taylor, James C. & Felten, David F. (1993). *Performance by Design: Sociotechnical Systems in North America.* Englewood Cliff, NJ: Prentice-Hall.

Tovey, M. J. (1984). Designing with Both Halves of the Brain. *Design Studies* 5(4):219-228.

Trist, Eric L. & Bamforth, Kenneth W. (1951). Some Social and Psychological Consequences of the Longwall Method of Coal Getting. *Human Relations.* 4:3-38.

Ulrich, W. (1983). *Critical Heuristics of Social Planning.* Berne, Belgium: Haupt.

University Associates, Inc. *Annuals for Facilitators, Trainers and Consultants.* San Diego, CA: Pfeiffer.

Ury, William L, Brett, Jeanne M. & Goldberg,

Stephen B. (1988). *Getting Disputes Resolved.* San Francisco, Jossey-Bass.

van Eijnaten, Frans M. (1993). *The Paradigm that Changed the Work Place.* Van Gorcum & Company.

Vance, Mike (Disney) (1993). *Creative Thinking* (audio). Chicago: Nightingale Conant.

Van Oech, Roger (1983). *A Whack on the Side of the Head.* New York: Warner Books.

Von Oech, Roger (1986). *A Kick in the Seat of the Pants.* New York: Harper & Row.

Webber, James B.; Smith, Douglas M.; Novokowsky, Bernie J. & McWhinney, Will (1992). *Paths of Change Handbook.* Unpublished.

Webber, James B. (1991). *Facilitating Critical Thinking.* Unpublished.

Weihrich, H. (1982). The TOWS Matrix—A Tool for Situational Analysis. *Long Range Planning.* 15(2).

Weisbord, Marvin, et. al. (1992). *Discovering Common Ground.* San Francisco, CA: Jossey-Bass.

Ziegler, Warren L. (1982). *A Mindbook of Exercises for Future Invention.* Denver: Future Invention Associates.

THE AUTHORS

Will McWhinney (Ph.D. Carnegie-Mellon University) is a designer, consultant, and educator. His varied career began in the early 1950's with the Bell System designing computer and operations research applications. In the early 1960's he helped organize the business school at Leeds University (England) and was there introduced to the design of Socio-Technical Systems. He then joined in creating the first American STS program at the UCLA Graduate School of Management. By the 1970's he was working with the earliest of the high-performing open system organizations in manufacturing plants and in community development. In 1980 he helped found at the Fielding Institute in Santa Barbara the innovative doctoral program in Human and Organizational Systems for mid-career professionals. During the 1990's his work has lead to innovations in the theory and practice of social change. He is past president of the Association for Humanistic Psychology and Vice-President of International Synergy. Currently he heads his own consulting organization and can be contacted at:

Enthusion, Inc.
589 Grand Boulevard
Venice, CA 90291.
(310) 392-1343; FAX (310) 396-0675

James Webber is an independent management consultant specializing in strategic thinking, organizational renewal and inter-organizational collaboration for health care organizations. He holds an MBA from Harvard. Jim can be contacted at: 9 Wild Pasture Road, Kensington, NH 03827. (603) 772-5959.

Doug Smith is a partner in Organomics, Inc. a consulting firm in Calgary, Alberta, focused on the effectiveness of organizations. He is a senior organizational effectiveness specialist with operational and strategic expertise in planning, design, and change process. Doug's creative conceptual thinking has successfully helped clients in Canada and the United States translate ideas into bottom line results. He can be contacted at (403) 245-6780.

Bernie Novokowsky is a senior consultant, specializing in designing and implementing better organizational processes, systems, and outcomes. Strategic thinking, business acumen, and change mastery are core to his practice. He has amassed a record of successes in improving business results. Bernie is completing his Ph.D. in Organizational Systems from the Fielding Institute. His consulting firm is based in Calgary and works internationally. Bernie can be contacted at:
(403) 283-9185; FAX: (403) 283-2055
E-Mail: bernie@ncginc.com

NOTES:

NOTES:

NOTES:

NOTES: